Gare

As a valuable, true
friend of Dwight
Staten, you have
a special place in
my circle of acquaintances.
Your helpfulness, integrity,
& reliability to those
in need is greatly
appreciated.

Stay true to your
values, my brother.
Continued blessings,
Satan 4/17/2016

In Quest of That Elusive Thing Called a J O B

FROM AN INSIDER'S PERSPECTIVE

SOLARI JENKINS

authorHOUSE®

AuthorHouse™
1663 Liberty Drive
Bloomington, IN 47403
www.authorhouse.com
Phone: 1 (800) 839-8640

Published by AuthorHouse 01/07/2016

ISBN: 978-1-5049-7113-3 (sc)
ISBN: 978-1-5049-7105-8 (hc)
ISBN: 978-1-5049-7114-0 (e)

Print information available on the last page.

Any people depicted in stock imagery provided by Thinkstock are models, and such images are being used for illustrative purposes only. Certain stock imagery © Thinkstock.

This book is printed on acid-free paper.

CONTENTS

Part 4

ACKNOWLEDGMENTS

I want to acknowledge my wife, Hollis, who helped me get better organized and gave me gentle reminders when I struggled to stay on track, my daughters Alycsa and Hollye, who offered encouragement and support whenever I reached out to them and to my step-daughter, Ashley Johnson, whose work ethic and focus is refreshing to see in a young adult. In addition, there are countless friends, extended family-members, acquaintances and colleagues who inspired my development over the years, on many levels. I'd like to mention some of them who either assisted or inspired me in this project… probably in ways they will never know. They include: my God-Niece Natalia Allsop, who did the wonderful illustration for the cover, my stepgranddaughter Dorica Romain, who proves that persistence and faith will win out over setbacks, Dawson Leong, Hamid Habibvand, Anita Kumari, Craig Cuffie, Alan Laird, Marsha Foster, James Ratliff, Jon Gundersgaard, Richard Mullins, Bobby King, Kevin Meltone, Octave Baker, Fr. Kwame, Fr. Aidan, Fr. Jay, Fr. Hilary, and my St. Columba church family, Christine Nichols, Dwight Staten, Darryl Bozeman, Sister Monica, Annie Chan, Annette Atkins, Alfred Garcia, Eugenia Perkins, Jaune McClenton, Paul Hancock, Tarabu Betserai-Kirkland, Ben Bowser, Shana Hudson, Phelicia Jones, Haifeng Wang, Chauncey Roberts, Sola Sobayo, Herb Pearl, Patrick Kabangu, Joe Compton, Sam Williams, Joe Richardson, Ricardo Scales, Thomas Steward, Herman Collins, Bernhard Hiller, George "Lefty" Smith, Al Banks, Dwight "Chi-town Flash" Lewis, Hulannie Jenkins, William Pegg, Shams Tabrez, Adrea Bailey, John Zissel, Pavel Stoffel, Sean Rouse, Ben Pope, Andy Anderson, Nunyo Zigah, Linda Bader, Tony Allsop, Imani Jackson, Yancie Taylor, Wilbert Lee, Teddy Strong, Wilbert Ross, Clinton Reynolds, William Hollis, John & Mary Battle, Sam & Karen Stewart, Conway Jones, Frank Jorden, Carol

Solari Jenkins

McMillan, Carol Ann Bishop, Marrgo Bjornsen, Lil Brown-Parker, Steve Jeffrey, Jimmy Williams, Ellie Chapman, Elsworth Lear, Michael Haugh, Joe Chiaramonte, J.J. Bola and the helpful, nice folks at Author House: Fred Trueblood, Allie Ireland, Phillip Scuderi, and Rhea Nolan. Thank you all!

PREFACE

There are always periods of time when jobs and opportunities appear to be scarce or in short supply. Although that is the case for some, it is a good reason to be equipped with as much knowledge, education, and experience you can muster in order to take your place among the employed, rather than to be on the outside looking in. I have put to paper what I believe to be valuable information that most serious-minded job seekers or career climbers should know as they race toward their goals. As you will soon learn, I believe that good results come from proper preparation. We usually want the best of things like the best school, the best project, the best job, the best car, and even the best marriage, but are we willing to do what is necessary to obtain them? Are we willing to invest the time, resources, and energy into ourselves? Sure, we buy the things we want that give us instant gratification, but what about the investment necessary to ensure a life of fulfillment while contributing to society in the manner of our choosing and training? To put it another way, working at something that we are passionate about is what many people seek, whether they know it or not.

Too often, we rush toward appealing career opportunities that we *know* we can do, only to be told that we are not qualified. Sometimes, you might be told that you are overqualified. What does that mean? Does it mean that you would do the job better than the employer would want it done? It can mean lots of things. For example, the employer may think you would be bored shortly after taking the job and would actively look for another opportunity with more challenge. Other explanations could be that your background appears to be at the level of the person that the job reports to and that person wouldn't feel comfortable having your level of experience reporting to them. Or based on your résumé, you could be more expensive than what they want to pay.

Many times, the "overqualified" response is trotted out whenever your background is not quite a fit but appears to be impressive. One of the advantages of a face-to-face interview or even a brief encounter at a job fair is that you get to speak directly to someone who can give you instant feedback on your résumé and qualifications for a job. In addition, a competent hiring person can often direct you to, or make a suggestion about, a more appropriate level or even a different job that matches your background better. Until that happens, however, you must invest the time and energy to do that for yourself. You will learn how to do a number of key things that will better prepare you for what you want and how to effectively utilize what you have already prepared yourself for in school or in your career.

So what should you do first? Well, you should learn what's in store for you process-wise as you embark upon your quest to get that career opportunity, job, or position you want.

Buckle your seat belt, and let's begin.

WHY I WROTE THIS BOOK

More times than I can remember, I would give helpful advice or answer job seekers' questions and they would emphatically thank me. My response often was "Aww, don't mention it. I do so gladly because I probably won't write a book about any of this stuff." Then one day, I thought, *Why* not *write a book about it?* There are many people who would like a better job, while there are others who would like a job period! Both groups need to know how to go about getting what they want. I've seen blogs, magazine articles, and reports on the Internet about job seeking techniques. I've seen employment sites that include helpful tips on a variety of topics that should assist job seekers, but I haven't seen anything in any one book that gives staffing info at this level from an insider's perspective. The subjects covered in this book are relevant and factual, and I trust helpful.

Read carefully, and enjoy!

Part 1

Chapter 1

THE HIRING PROCESS

People get invited to interviews by being referred by someone who is a friend who knows someone at a company that is hiring. He or she could be a professional contact of someone who works there, or this individual could be a college professor or school counselor who has a relationship with the company and routinely refers top students who demonstrate that they are bright, responsible, and consistently doing outstanding work. (What does this point out for you? Answer: the power of contacts and favorable impressions.)

Other ways to get invited to an interview are to apply for a position online and have either the staffing person (recruiter) or a sourcer contact you. A sourcer is a person who constantly searches the Internet, job boards, and his or her company's internal system for possible candidates for particular openings. However, hiring managers themselves may also contact you because one of your contacts could have gone directly to them in your regard. Search firms and temporary agencies, who are assisting their client companies fill jobs, are also advertising positions in a variety of ways: on their websites, on university websites (typically each department has its own), with banner or streaming ads on social media websites, in industry magazines, in the business section of local newspapers, and sometimes in newsletters that reach their intended audience.

Prior to the Interview

Get as much information as you can about the position you will be interviewing for, whether it's an internship or a regular position. Typically, the staffing or HR person will be able to furnish such info. If not, the hiring manager surely will. Sometimes, the first interactive contact with an employer is the phone interview—or the "phone screen" as it's referred to by the insiders (i.e., staffing people and hiring managers). It is just that—a screening. Someone is interested in your résumé or background but needs to ask some clarifying questions before inviting you in for a face-to-face interview. Occasionally, the phone screen may be conducted via a teleconference call, Skype, or something similar where you will be visible to the interviewer. Please do not take this convenient usage of technology too casually. Remember that it is a business activity, so dress appropriately and not in your pajamas or some other inappropriate attire.

Let me give you a little inside tip here. There are times when a candidate is scheduled to receive a phone call, but it doesn't happen. After your preparation, anticipation, and patience waiting to discuss your background and whatever else, the phone doesn't ring. To safeguard against this disappointment, make sure you ask the person who schedules the phone interview for an additional name or contact just in case something comes up that prevents that person from phoning you at the appointed time. This helps to reinforce the verbal commitment because no employee wants their boss or colleague to know that they were so negligent that they stood up a candidate and a potential addition to their company. And to be honest, things do come up that throw a wrench into the best of intentions.

Be Prepared

Go over your résumé beforehand and anticipate what areas may be of interest to them, given what you know about the job or the company. Have it handy in case you need to discuss dates or the chronology of your experience and why you made job changes when you did. Be aware that they may have people there who know of you or the group or department you worked in at XYZ Company, which can be either good or bad. The hiring manager or the person conducting the phone screen may have left for the same reasons that you did. Be honest, but do not bash a former employer. Most employers realize that not every environment is suitable for every employee, regardless of their skill level.

Study the job description and create possible questions they might ask you about your background, experience, or education that matches the position. Naturally, it's also helpful to know something about the company, their industry, and even their products; it could also perhaps be useful to have knowledge of a new product introduction or a recent merger or acquisition they recently completed. Some companies may have added key services or broadened the network of customers they serve, while others may have expanded internationally.

The better informed a candidate is about the company they are interviewing with, the better their chances of doing well. Although rare, sometimes the impossible happens. Sometimes, a candidate who was not thought to be the leading candidate, based on his or her résumé, comes into the interview so well prepared—with functional information about the company, its competitors, its market challenges, and what products the company should be focusing on to improve its market share—that he or she is now suddenly catapulted to the top and gets the job! As the great former heavyweight champion of the world said,

> Impossible is just a big word thrown around by small men who find it easier to live in the world they've been given than to explore the power they have to change it. Impossible is not a fact. It's an opinion. Impossible is not a declaration. It's a dare. Impossible is potential. Impossible is temporary. Impossible is nothing.

—Muhammad Ali

Develop Your Questions

Since the interviewer or interviewers (since sometimes it's a panel interview, which we'll get to later) are going to ask most of the questions, the interviewee (that's you!) needs to ensure that he or she gets his or her own questions in during the interview. I would suggest you write several good questions down before you get there.

Go over them as if you were memorizing a poem or a song lyric. In short, have them become natural for you. Questions about salary, time off, vacation, and benefits should be reserved for the staffing person, who usually goes over benefits and will possibly have the salary discussion with you when appropriate. Your questions should be about the position (i.e., expectations of the job, specific areas to focus on that would help the group succeed, organizational structure (organizational chart), reporting structure, and future opportunities to learn and expand your knowledge and experience). It is always appropriate to inquire as to how long the interviewer has worked there and what they find most rewarding and, conversely, most challenging. You might be curious about the reason this position is available. This could be a good indicator of the complexity or importance of the job—or even your potential upward mobility.

Now that you are armed with info about the position, the company, and your possible questions, you are ready to go into the interview with confidence and enthusiasm. Yes, enthusiasm! Attitude plays a big part in the hiring process. Companies want go-getters who demonstrate their enthusiasm to learn and to become contributing members of their organization. You are interviewing to become part of a company, group, division, department, team, project, or program, so demonstrating your enthusiasm and your ability to easily interact with others is very important.

Dress for Success

Before proceeding, let me mention that for each interview you go on, you should be in business attire. Women should wear a business suit or skirt with a blazer, and men should dress in a business suit or in a sports coat with dress slacks. Remember this is business, not a casual meeting with your friends or relatives. When you dress in business attire, you demonstrate that you are serious about this process and that you respect it and the people whose time you will take up to interview you. Remember the old adage of getting one shot at making a good first impression? Well, your appearance is that first impression. Plus each of those interviewers already works there and has responsibilities to get back to once the interview is over. See that they return to work with a positive impression of you and your ability to do the job! (For those companies where everyone dresses in jeans and casual attire, you can dress casually also—once you work there.)

The Interview

If there are introductions and handshaking, please give a firm handshake and look the person directly in the face or eyes as you speak. Ladies, your handshake should be firm and as businesslike as any of your male competitors for this career opportunity. Do not offer a limp, uninspired, dead fish of a handshake to start the beginning of what could very well be the most important position of your career. Sit up and sit at the front edge of the chair—this is no time to slouch or slump down in the chair. There is nothing casual about interviews; they can be pleasant, but not casual.

Answer each question clearly and completely without rambling on and on. Be ready to demonstrate an answer by writing on a white board or by showing graphs, charts, or other results from a project you did that is relevant to the subject. Please ask an interviewer to restate or to (please) repeat a question that you don't understand. Never wing it to pretend that you know what was said and hope your answer is correct. For those of you in the engineering arena, oftentimes engineers will ask you to solve a problem—not so much to have you solve it but to observe your thought process and the way you approach a problem. As you know, it could be a circuit or a leading-edge process. Or in some cases, if you are a recent grad, they may have requested you to prepare a presentation about the area you will be working in. In that case, you would have been presenting during the first part of your interview schedule and will get a sense of what questions will be asked later based on the Q&A portion during your presentation.

Be honest and answer questions truthfully. If you are familiar with a particular system or concept but never worked with it, say so. It makes sense to say, "I haven't worked on it, but I'm familiar with it and confident I can learn it rather quickly." If you don't think you were clear in your answer at any time during the interview, say, "Let me go back to that question for a minute because I forgot to mention." Or say, "I'm not sure I was as clear as I could be, so let me restate that answer for you." Do not walk out of an interview and later regret that you didn't say something essential on a particular topic.

After the interviewer has asked all of the questions and you have asked and received answers to yours, finish the interview by asking if there are other questions the interviewer has for you. If not, take this time to express your continued interest in this career opportunity. (Should you not want to go forward, it is appropriate to state that as well. Sometimes, during the interviews, it becomes apparent that the job is not what you thought it was and you are no longer interested or you realize that you are not qualified to do it.)

If there were several different interviews and this one is the last interview for the day, it is appropriate to ask the next steps. "Will there be subsequent interviews, and when do you anticipate making a decision on hiring for this position?" This is a good time to mention if you are interviewing at other companies or are anticipating an offer from another employer. By sharing this information, you are giving them an opportunity to get back to you in a timely manner before you accept another position that they were unaware of. Generally, an HR or staffing person would ask if you are interviewing at other companies, but if not, this is important information to share.

After the Interview

Usually with larger companies, each person who interviews will produce a business card with their contact information on it. If not, request contact information from the person who set up the interview or from the staffing or human resources person. Within twenty-four hours, you want to send a follow-up "Thank you for your time" email message to each of the people you met with during the interview schedule. (A phone call left in their voice mailbox is appropriate as well.) This follow-up also gives you an opportunity to reiterate your interest in the position and to reinforce why you would be a good fit for it. Candidates have said things like

> After meeting with you and the other interview team members yesterday, and based on my education and experience, I feel confident that I could both contribute to, and learn from, your organization—while working at what I enjoy doing most.

Candidates have also said,

> I really appreciate the time you spent describing the position and the challenges of it with me yesterday. I feel confident that I am up for the challenge, and I can assure you that I will work very hard to learn all I can to quickly become a contributing member of the team.

There are others who have been brief and to the point, saying, "I enjoyed the time we spent together yesterday and I really want the job." Or "I liked everything I heard and I'm looking forward to working with you."

If there is a question that you think you could have answered better with a particular interviewer, feel free to revisit it with them to give a more comprehensive answer. Be open to any follow-up, more in-depth questioning from them, because they've had time to think about it also. One sticking point could be the difference between getting a yes vote from an interviewer and a no vote, which could be the deciding opinion of you getting the job or not.

And although it pains me to say so, there are interviewers who will ding a candidate for something they didn't bother to ask them. During postinterview discussions to evaluate interviewees' capabilities for the job (sometimes called round-table discussions or candidate evaluations), there are interviewers who might say, "I'm not sure so-and-so has solid knowledge of x." Well, if that reckless thought isn't checked by someone asking if they had explored that subject with the interviewee, and if it is an important component of the job, that candidate may be torpedoed by someone who didn't do a thorough job of interviewing.

One should not be dinged for something that was assumed he or she didn't know! This is a good reason why thorough and complete answers should be given during an interview. Seldom do we experience a whole team of interviewers who conduct good, thorough interviews. Even in smaller companies where the boss of the company does all the hiring, they seldom are adept at proper interview techniques and generally depend on their gut feelings in making their hiring decisions. Too often, those decisions are made with little objectivity but subjectively—and can sometimes be discriminatory and biased. Yes, gender, racial, and age discrimination or biases do exist. (I was dismayed some months ago when I read that a woman having lunch in a restaurant in Toronto overheard executives from one of the largest corporations in the world state that they "aren't hiring young women because they just get pregnant again and again." I'm sure that sentiment isn't the prevailing view within that company, but it's just another example of the negative, backward-thinking biases of some people in this modern age. And I thought the Neanderthals had died off. How disgusting.)

There are laws to protect us from such actions, but such biases still exist and rear their ugly heads by preventing us from getting positions that we should have gotten. (Several times, I felt like I was rushed through the interview by people who seemed to be only going through the motions with no intention of hiring me. While other situations, after getting hired and realizing that certain key people whom I *had* to work with seemed disinterested in working with me by being slow to accept a proposed scheduled time to meet with me or reluctant to return my calls to set up meetings to go over their openings. I found myself faced with an uphill battle as soon as I started working there.

Since I was hired to fill all of the openings in that group, including those in their department, I certainly intended to do just that. Like most pros, I hung in there, quickly learned as much as I could about their area of responsibility, put forth whatever effort it took to learn the company's processes, systems and procedures, and developed creative ways to meet with those hiring managers who were too busy to meet with me during normal business hours. I would often show up at their offices during their lunchtime or after normal work hours, whenever I could catch them. And later, with good follow-through, turning up good candidates and demonstrating an unrelenting desire to fill each critical opening with top talent in a timely manner, supported by good results, I was able to dispel their negative stereotypes or false impressions and was able to establish good working relationships. Although my focus was to work and do the very best job I could, over time, several friendships developed, complete with lunch invitations.

I remember starting a job on a Friday so that the departing recruiter could take me around and introduce me to some of the hiring managers that I would be working with, while he said his good-byes on his last day. Well, the first one went okay, although the person was surprised and sorry to hear that he was leaving. He smiled during our introduction, shook my hand, and welcomed me aboard. The second stop was at a corner office of a director who seemed to be quite busy on his computer. After we waited outside his office for a few minutes, my colleague, the departing recruiter, while still outside of the office, told him that today was his last day and that I was his replacement. The director quickly approached us, reached out to my colleague pulling him into his office, and closed the door in my face! I guess he was really surprised and not very pleased hearing such news. After waiting a short time, feeling a bit out of sorts in a new environment, not knowing anyone, and looking like I was lost, I found a water fountain and took a short stroll around the area. Once my colleague returned, say five minutes or so (but which seemed like an eternity!), he apologized and said that he hadn't bothered to tell any of the directors of the groups he supported because he didn't want to disappoint them. He suggested we go and meet more people. I replied, "No, I'm good. I think I can take it from here." As you might have guessed, I had to later work closely with hiring managers in that director's group. About six or seven months later, he singled me out during one of his staff meetings for having done an "outstanding job" of hiring a number of key people in his organization. He and I hardly ever met, so I don't know if he remembered my first day and our first encounter or not.

After you've done the things mentioned earlier, such as following up with a thank-you, seeing if you need to revisit a question or two, and letting them know that you definitely are confident that you can do and want the job, you aren't finished until you get the job. You want to follow up on a regular basis. Be tenacious about wanting to get the job; ask if there is something else needed from your end. Perhaps, they aren't clear on your particular knowledge on something that you know very well and need to have you address. When you follow up on a consistent basis, you are keeping your candidacy alive and you are demonstrating your desire to work there. (Remember they cannot assume that you are still interested or still available unless you let them know.)

Let's summarize what we've covered.

We want to do our research to find out what we can learn about the job, the company, and its industry. With what we know, we want to develop several questions about the position. We want to dress appropriately and have an upbeat, enthusiastic attitude. We want to give clear and thorough answers to interview questions.

Please follow up with an email, voice mail, or some form of communication after the interview.

Chapter 2

WHAT IS GOING ON?
I CAN'T GET ANYONE TO
RETURN MY CALLS

Knowing that each opening is critical to the successful function of a company, when the finalist candidate is identified, immediate attention and focus is placed on them. If you are not the "final" candidate, you may not hear from the company until that person has accepted or turned down the job.

So instead of telling you the job has been filled when it hasn't yet, you may not get any communication until they know the final outcome. This practice from the non-chosen candidates' standpoint may seem a bit unfair, but from the company's view, it is quite appropriate. There have been many instances when a company thought it had a position filled, only to have the candidate decide to take another job or say they were moving out of state because their spouse accepted a job offer that was too good to turn down! Another backbreaking interruption in completing a hire that comes to mind is when a candidate has been offered a job, delays giving their decision for a week or more, decides to decline the offer, and stays put with their current employer. (I will spend more time later discussing the counter offer.)

The company then has to go back to the second-place or even third-place candidate to see if they are still available or still interested in the position. If considerable time has elapsed and they are no longer available, the staffing people will have to start the process all over again. Just think: if this was a critical opening when it was first opened weeks or months ago, it has become even more critical since so much time has passed. Now there is ramped-up pressure put on the hiring manager and the staffing people to fill it as quickly as possible! If the staffing person is working on some sort of bonus per hire or has a monthly goal to fill a certain number of hires, having to start over could be very detrimental to their job and to their income. If a recruiter or staffing consultant is ineffective in filling openings in a timely manner, they won't be around very long!

Sometimes the brakes are put on a hiring decision because the position is put on hold for any number of business reasons. Oftentimes it would be because of a reorganization where they halt all hiring until the dust settles. There could be budget changes, since the new employee will be put on the payroll and will receive company benefits—they obviously must be budgeted for before coming on board.

What also happens with some frequency is a change in leadership, where the new leader needs time to assess her human resources in her new role. She must decide where she should prioritize her hiring focus. But one of the most impactful occurrences that can halt everything is the dreaded *f* word: a hiring *freeze.* No one wants to even hear the term freeze uttered, because it signals bad things. Not only will hiring cease for a while, but typically, a layoff or a RIF (reduction in force) accompanies a freeze or follows soon after. If a hiring freeze is scheduled for a protracted amount of time, it is quite possible that the arrogant-sounding HR or staffing person who seemed so curt in their communication with you when you were unemployed and really needed a job badly, and seldom returned your phone calls or emails, saying that they were very busy, just might be joining you in the ranks of the unemployed. Especially if they are contract recruiters and not regular employees. It is all the more likely if the hiring freeze is set to last for several months or longer, because staffing professionals (recruiters, etc.) are brought on board specifically to fill jobs.

The longer a company has a hiring freeze, the more insecure their employees become. They start looking over their shoulders to see if they are going to be notified of being laid off or "riffed." They become paranoid and wonder if they are next. Company morale suffers and occasionally cooperation suffers too, because a segment of the employee population wants to be viewed as indispensable. They begin taking sole credit for things that they did or did not completely do on their own. I've seen fellow employees challenged unnecessarily during staff meetings so that the questioner looks good to their boss. And I've seen team members taking credit for good ideas they received from other employees outside of their organization's inner circle. And worse: employees pointing fingers or blaming others for something that didn't go well. Definitely, the worse comes out when the potential for losing one's job is in the air. Teamwork and sharing credit for success as a team goes out the window! Typically, upper management doesn't allay their fears by reassuring large population of employees that they have nothing to be concerned about. Perhaps they aren't sure themselves!

As I said, hiring freezes are never good for long periods of time. Yet there are instances where only a department or a division of a company might have a hiring freeze while the rest of the company conducts business as usual, complete with accelerated hiring in many disciplines! Yet some hiring freezes last just long enough to get an accounting of the number of positions and to confirm the budget to fill them.

Those are just some of the reasons why it sometimes takes a long time to get feedback after interviewing. Naturally, sudden illnesses and other unplanned PTO (personal time off) by key decision-makers can also slow down the process and cause delays in making decisions. I've worked with groups where the department head would frequently designate someone to go forward in such cases. But on the other hand, I know of department heads and other senior-level types who would designate someone to handle everything in their absence except their hiring decisions! If you can establish good rapport with your staffing or HR contact who you call regularly, they will most likely give you the real skinny on what's going on. That is, if they have the time or bandwidth to return your calls.

When a company is in the midst of an accelerated hiring phase, your staffing person or HR contact could be swamped with so much activity that they cannot get back to you or anyone else in a timely manner. And if their priorities have changed, they could be working in a different area than the one you interviewed for and recruiting for openings completely different. (I can recall times when I had to keep late office hours just to respond to candidates who had interviewed and needed feedback. I knew the importance of providing such input, especially if the position was put on hold or was to be suspended for a protracted amount of time. Once that area was put on hold, I would be given new priorities, which meant I'd have to meet with and start working with hiring managers in a different organization—with different requirements of critical openings that needed my attention right then! Another equally conscientious and talented staffing colleague and a dear friend, Jon Gundersgaard, would instruct his candidates to contact him if they received no information in a few days. He'd say, "If you don't hear anything from us, call me back and I'll tell you what is going on." Jon obviously had been through several stop-and-go and staffing reassignment scenarios before, but he understood the importance of timely communication.)

If the candidate was in no rush and could wait, that was fine. But if they were ready to make a move or needed a job right away, this information would be most important to them and their family.

Regardless of where you may be in the hiring process, until you get a job, stay abreast of what's occurring in your chosen field. Attend professional association events and job fairs, participate in online discussions about your areas of interest, and read whatever related journals and blogs you can find. Also continue networking and searching for other opportunities that match what you want to do. Expand your network of friends and acquaintances. The more people who know you are a talented person trying to get a job, the better your chances of getting one. I recently saw part of an interview of Wendy Spencer, CEO of the Corporation for National and Community Service (CNCS), which is a "federal agency that engages more than five million Americans in service through its core programs—Senior Corps, AmeriCorps, and the Social Innovation Fund ..." She said something of interest regarding employment. She said that a research study on volunteering showed that "when you volunteer, you increase the odds of getting a job by 27 percent." She went on to say that when you volunteer your services, management at those companies gets to see your skills, how you work with others, and your dedication and reliability. And based on those observations and having gotten to know you, they feel comfortable offering you a regular salaried job as soon as they have an opening. She also said that by volunteering, you get the chance to gain experience in areas that you hadn't worked in before. So as they say in educational circles, my takeaway from that interview was to definitely add volunteering to the list of ways to get a regular job.

LinkedIn, among some other social networking sites for business professionals, has become one of the most widely used recruiting tools in a number of top companies. The staffing people at those companies are encouraged to post their openings—those jobs they are responsible for filling—on LinkedIn and to search for candidates there as well. In some companies, Monster.com, craigslist, Zip Recruiter, CareerBuilder, and a host of social media sites are used to find people. (I'm sure you've heard this, but just to reinforce the point, be careful what you put on your social media pages because displaying inappropriate images of yourself and engaging in improper commentary or other demonstrations of poor judgment can and will come back to bite you on your proverbial backside! So be aware and be careful.)

A Quick Recap

Sometimes when you hear nothing after an interview, it may not have anything to do with you.

If you have a good relationship with your contact at the company, you have a better chance of getting timely information regarding business-driven delays.

Volunteer while you are still looking for that right, regular job.

Utilize social media sites, especially those for business professionals.

Chapter 3

IF YOU ARE CHOSEN FOR THE JOB

After you get the call that you have been selected, the references and background check processes begin. Make sure that your references are fully aware of your interview, the position you interviewed for, and who might be calling. Also, be sure to have current contact information for each of your references so that they can be reached easily. It's a good idea to have additional references in case some of your top five are unavailable. Regarding the background check, whatever you filled out on your application form is open to scrutiny. If you completed all of your core courses but never actually received your degree, please do not put on your résumé as completed and received. Although it is important to present accurate data, it is sometimes difficult to remember all of your dates accurately, but do your best to recall them. (It is suggested to have your résumé handy to double-check.) If you need to change or clarify something you put on your application, please alert your company contact and have them walk you through what you need to do. Leave nothing up to chance because chances are it won't serve you well if you should have changed something.

After you have successfully passed the background check and your references have not torpedoed you or your chances of getting this wonderful career opportunity, the offer is next. Once you've accepted the job and agreed to a salary or compensation package (we'll discuss this a little later on), you'll need to establish a start date. A start date that will give you time to complete your pressing personal affairs so that you will give yourself the best opportunity to devote your energy and attention to your new job, while keeping in mind that you need to start as soon as you can. Once you start, oftentimes on a Monday, you will participate in the company's orientation and sign up for the company benefits for yourself and your dependents; information needs to be understood, decisions made, and forms filled out. Show up well rested and alert.

Realizing that everyone working there is ahead of you because they know the formal systems and procedures, how things really get done, know a number of the go-to people, and may be familiar with the politics that exist, you will need to put in the time and effort it takes to catch up. If that means coming in a little earlier and staying later than your colleagues, then do so. Not only will you come up to speed quickly, you will also get the respect of your colleagues and management with your work ethic and the knowledge you will gain. Plus you'll put your career growth on the fast track and find yourself given more responsibility and experience upward mobility, sooner rather than later.

If You Are Not Chosen for the Job

If you get the call that you were not selected for the job, ask what you were deficient in so that you can improve for the next interview you have. If the response is something specific that you can improve on, go do so. Ask if there are other positions that might match your background and skill level. And if they anticipate other openings that you might qualify for, ask if you could check in with them from time to time or if you need to contact someone else who may be responsible for those positions. If they are fine with you touching base with them on a regular basis, do so. (I have experienced this and know it to be an effective way to pursue a job you want. There were instances where candidates would check in with me on the very day that I'd been notified of an opening that matched their background!)

While you are still in the market for a job, network with your friends, schoolmates, and past instructors/trainers/professors who may remember you and know of your work. The more people who know you are job searching and who know of your level of commitment and work ethic, the better your chances of getting an interview and getting hired. Remember those business cards you received from the interviewers? Reach out to the ones you felt you connected well with, had good rapport with, or had something in common with, because they know people as well. Also, go about your normal routine, especially if you have hobbies or interests where you may interact with other people.

Back in the spring when the weather was warm and trees were in bloom with vibrant shades of green leaves and some flowers, I decided to go window-shopping along one of my favorite streets in Albany, California, which is near Berkeley. Well, as I looked into the windows at assortments of everything from clothing to dust pans and things for the maintenance of the home, I saw the most incredible lamps in a small lamp store! As I drew closer to the windows, I saw the small tickets dangling off them and stating, "Hand-painted." There were all shapes and sizes of lamps with very creatively designed and hand-painted lampshades. Upon entering the store, I was greeted by an attractive woman with a very nice smile. I spoke with her for a few minutes and began to look at the wonderful lamps and most unique-looking lampshades. I later told her how I was drawn in by the shades and that they were the most unusual but appealing lamps I had seen in quite some time. I told her that I was recently retired and what I had done as a profession. I asked if she had been working there long, expecting her to say about five years or more since she was so knowledgeable and so enthusiastic about the store and its products. She then told me her story.

She had been window shopping and was drawn into the store because of the beautifully painted lampshades and the great-looking lamps with so much character and variety. Well, as she spoke with the owner of the business, gushing over the way the lamps and the overall energy of the place made her feel, the owner asked what kind of work she did. She said that she wasn't working at the time, having recently completed a temporary assignment in an administrative capacity and was in fact still mulling over what she wanted to do next. To her astonishment, yet delight, the owner offered her a job on the spot! She said it was the best job she has had in years, doing what she really enjoys and being in a place filled with creativity and beautiful things. On top of all of that, she loved her boss and they got along like they'd known each other for years. And that had all happened only two months ago!

Get the Job Meant for You

As some job seekers have mentioned, it is just as much work looking for work as it is working, and in some cases, it is more work. But when you devote the proper amount of time and effort to your job search, the more your professional network will grow. And it stands to reason that the larger your network, the greater the odds of you getting connected to that job you are seeking.

So what is the key to successfully getting that career opportunity you want? Hold on to your hat. Wait for it.

It is to properly PREPARE.

- Proceed. Put your thoughts into action.
- Research. Do background work on the company and its industry.
- Evaluate best approaches to take.
- Position yourself to succeed.
- Accept your shortcomings and work to improve.
- Reflect on past challenges and successes.
- Engage in associations and activity that involve and support your objective.

Now let's proceed and begin our proper preparation.

Part 2

Chapter 4

PREPARATION

In preparing to secure a job or a position working for someone else, you must first properly prepare.

Prepare your résumé to show what you've done but also state what you want to do.

Prepare yourself for the rejection that surely comes.

Prepare yourself for interviews.

Prepare yourself for closing the deal on the job you want.

To paraphrase a popular saying, "He who fails to prepare is preparing to fail."

Once you've agreed that preparation is the cornerstone of landing the job of your dreams or the position that will launch your career or the one that will enable you to provide for you and your family, then proceed.

Mind-set Preparation

Like anything worth having, you must resolve to give it your all and not waste your time or anyone else's time on this quest. Remember these are highly competitive times. There are people from around the globe competing for your job. The brainiacs who were shunned in your social circles but who made the A's while you struggled to earn your B's are after what you're after. Like any other competition, positioning and follow-through are essential to succeeding.

Rejection

Yes, prepare for it. It will happen, without a doubt. Thomas Edison's response, when asked if he was crestfallen because he had failed to make the light bulb work after one hundred attempts, was "Not at all." He said, "I now know one hundred ways it won't work." And he went on to say that he knew he was "that much closer." I am not suggesting that it will take one hundred or more attempts for you to land the job of your choice, but be prepared to have several tries at it. As the saying goes, "For every no, a yes is that much closer."

Rejection will appear in many forms: your résumé gets passed over as not being a good fit for the job, or you hurriedly put a résumé together by regurgitating your current and former job descriptions with little thought of including any outcome or impact that your efforts contributed to the success of the company. Those job descriptions tell the prospective employer very little about your performance. If your résumé does its job and you are called for a phone interview, it may not go as you'd hoped. Maybe your answers to certain key questions were thought to be unspecific or unclear; if you interviewed in person, you might have done really well with a couple of the interviewers but not do so well with the hiring manager. You just couldn't read him or her and felt uncomfortable trying to figure out what they wanted to hear. And of course, there are times when you just can't think properly. You know that you know the answer, but it just won't come to you. Plus if you are nervous, the whole interview may be affected, and you may not recover. Or during an interview, whether over the telephone or in person, you come across as aloof or arrogant with little to back up your demeanor, such as having an absolutely stellar background of accomplishment and exceptional, in-depth knowledge of the areas pertinent to the job. You, my friend, have just flushed your chance of getting that job right down the drain.

It may come as a surprise to some people how important attitude and personality are in deciding who gets hired and who does not. Even in the most technical of positions, when education, knowledge, and experience are even, attitude more than likely wins out. Many times, I've heard hiring managers and other members of the interview team comment on a candidate's positive attitude—and how some others seemed uninterested or lacked enthusiasm about the work or the job in general.

Do Your Homework

A large part of preparing yourself for the entire hiring process is learning as much as you can about things connected to a job, company, or the industry that you are interested in pursuing. If you work at it by networking properly, you may be able to position yourself in what is called an exploratory or informational interview. It typically involves a candidate or job seeker meeting with a potential employer or hiring manager who may or may not have a current opening. The purpose is for the job seeker (you!) to gain information about a certain industry, company, department, or discipline that you wouldn't normally get from the company's website or from an advertisement and to establish a connection or a business relationship with an employer. These interviews differ from typical job interviews because they are not always about an existing job, or if they are, the job seeker may not be sure of the qualifications or requirements or may have doubts about meeting the qualifications. Exploratory interviews are effective ways to introduce yourself to a company that you are interested in working for and a way of getting in the door to discuss your abilities for possible employment. Also, in addition to reaching out to a hiring manager, if you can establish reasonable rapport with a staffing person and they have an open time slot, they too are good contacts for exploratory interviews.

Generally, exploratory or informational interviews occur when you are referred to someone in the company through a mutual acquaintance, a schoolteacher, or college professor, or even a counselor who knows of your work. Or you might be referred by someone related to an employee of the company, someone who actually works at the company who knows you, or even someone who previously interviewed at the company and thinks you would be a good fit but is not sure in what capacity. Staffing people ask people for referrals all the time. Maybe you readily come to mind when a staffing person asks someone you know for a referral to fill a key job of theirs. Maybe you come to mind because of your positive, professional manner! As you might imagine, I've granted many exploratory or informational interviews over the years. Let me share one with you that comes to mind.

Several years ago, I received a phone call around midmorning from an applicant who had seen our job posting on our website along with my name as the contact person. I was surprised to discover that the phone he was calling from was in our lobby, because I was very busy and hadn't scheduled any interviews that day until after lunch. As much as I tried to tell him how busy I was, he was nearly pleading with me to just give him five minutes and that he wouldn't waste my time with this interruption of my day. I was "busy as a long-tailed cat in a room full of rocking, rocking-chairs" in those days because I was the sole recruiter for the largest (and one of the busiest) divisions of the company, with many important and some hard-to-fill, critical openings that were keeping me hopping from early morning to early in the evening. (I often worked through lunch or ate at my desk and was too busy to accept lunch invitations from my boss! After my third decline of his invite, I shared with him that I could go to lunch with him or continue filling my critical openings in a timely manner while keeping the hiring managers and upper management happy, or I could go to lunch with him consistently and have things fall apart. He understood.)

As busy as I was, I couldn't honestly refuse a request from this applicant for just five minutes! Plus I was a bit curious to see if this guy was as good as he claimed to be.

After going to the lobby to meet him, signing him in, and escorting him to my office, I gave him the requested five minutes. He was well prepared. He had a copy of his résumé in hand, along with our job description of the position he was interested in, and he was nicely attired in a business suit and highly polished shoes. He thanked me for taking the time out of my busy day and proceeded to tell me why he was a good fit for the job by telling me about his background and experience and several outstanding accomplishments he had achieved while doing a very similar function with another company in our industry.

Although we talked for longer than five minutes, probably twelve to fifteen minutes, he didn't abuse the granted opportunity to meet with me. After listening intently to the pointed questions I directed at him, and responding with really good, thoughtful answers, I was convinced that he was indeed a good candidate for the position. Without skipping a beat, I called the hiring manager's office to set him up for an interview. So even though he had no appointment with me, he did have my name, and after getting me to give him a few minutes of my time, he came well prepared, was specific in what he wanted, and was able to demonstrate his qualifications for the job he wanted. (Yes, he was a marketing professional—to be exact, a product marketing manager candidate. And he not only got the job but later was promoted to director.)

Hiring Is Big Business

Remember companies are constantly adding to their candidate database because they are *always* in need of good talent. Even search-engine and job-board companies, whose business centers on posting résumés and selling the permission to search those résumés (to employers for their hiring needs), work tirelessly to develop systems that make it more attractive and easier to serve their customers. (Sites like LinkedIn, Monster, Dice, Zip Recruiter, and Indeed come to mind.) According to information posted on Monster.com's website that I saw recently (August 2015), it read,

> Every minute on Monster's worldwide network there are …
> 29 Résumés updated, 7,900 Jobs searched, 2,800 Jobs
> viewed.

As you can see, this is huge! Your résumé may be viewed by thousands of people around the world, and it will certainly be compared to many others in the process. You would want to ensure that it is the best representation of you, your background, and your highlighted, relevant accomplishments that you can produce.

Résumé Preparation

So here's what separates the successful candidates from the also-rans: your résumé is your calling card; but it can act as your business agent if prepared properly.

Before developing your résumé, first some steps must be undertaken and completed, such as these: skills and talent assessment, and deciding on what function or position within that function you are going after. For example, if you are interested in accounting, what position within the accounting function are you going after? Accounts payable, accounts receivable, cost accounting, general ledger, or finance and financial analysis? As you may know, there are many.

Skills and Talent Assessment

This process can be as difficult as anything for some, while easy as all get out for others. You must take stock of yourself. Go to a place where you do your best thinking: your home office, living room, deck, favorite coffee shop or bookstore, or room—wherever your thoughts flow or circulate within your mental grasp and you have uninterrupted space to focus. Think of the tasks, duties, and responsibilities that you enjoyed getting done and would enjoy doing again! Think of your fondest jobs: the company environments, the relationships you were able to establish, and the how or why you did certain things in your job. Don't forget the challenges you faced and the successes you experienced while being as tenacious and focused as you could possibly be to overcome the challenges you faced on a routine basis. Think of how you grew as a person who had to work well with people in other departments you didn't know but got to know and were able to depend on as they could depend on you. Remember how you were years ago compared to how you are now with presentations or functioning in a leadership role.

For those of you who haven't worked in the outside world yet but are now embarking upon that important quest to locate the right opportunity while having only school projects or part-time summer jobs to reflect on, think of the responsibilities you had as a project team member and how important your contribution was to the completion of those projects. Usually, project roles are divided by specialty areas where everyone is responsible for a component of the whole.

How critical was your part? Were you the project leader with responsibility to pull it all together? Did you coordinate your team's portion with another team off campus or in another state or country? Did your group partner with a company of professionals on something leading edge that may find its way into a product in the future?

Think of the responsibility of your part-time jobs. Did you have sole responsibility for anything? Were you required to keep track of anything, create reports, and develop any processes where you improved some of the company's procedures? If you worked in retail, did you have open and closing responsibilities? Did you train others? Did you have to work on a cash register and closely with customers? Did you train others in any capacity? What did you learn that whet your appetite for more involvement or stimulated you to expand your knowledge to do even more in your job?

I'm reminded of stories told to me by people who worked in jobs breaking their backs while seeing others do what appeared to be easy, stress-free work and how that compelled them to go back to finish their education in the hopes of getting one of the easier jobs. Just remember there are no shortcuts to success. Always do your best and invest in yourself by always learning and in becoming more proficient in whatever you do. Many very successful people pride themselves on continuously learning to stay current with the ever-changing technology, approaches, or methods of doing things better and simpler.

Not long ago, I saw Craig Bohl, the football coach of North Dakota State, being interviewed on television right after his team won the FCS Championship for the third year in a row. He was asked if he and his team were striving for perfection from the very beginning of the season. He replied, "When you strive for perfection, that won't happen, but along the way you're gonna catch excellence!")

While playing back these "tapes," reflect on your other growth patterns and how you were able to take on additional critical responsibilities with each new project, job, or promotion.

Note: If you apply yourself while in college or a university, there is the possibility of getting a summer internship that lasts until your classes resume in the fall. While working as an intern, you will have work responsibilities like the regular employees have at the company. You will attend meetings, create reports on the projects you are assigned to work on, and overall get a firsthand view of what it might be like to work in that capacity at that company. The internship opportunities generally are available to students in their junior year up to grad level and doctoral level. And yes, a significant number of former interns are offered full-time, regular positions after graduation. Internships are definitely a win-win program. Oftentimes, students returning to school in the fall, after completing an internship, have a better understanding of what they need to be more proficient in or what subjects they might want to spend more time on in order to be better prepared to succeed in their chosen field upon graduation. In addition to obtaining internships through school, some companies will advertise directly for intern talent via postings on their websites, other popular job boards, and by contacting certain alumni associations.

Selecting a Function or a Position within a Function

Contrary to public belief, the selection of your next career opportunity doesn't always have to be a specific job title. Let's say for conversation's sake that you are a recent grad, have a degree in marketing, and have been led to believe that you are aptly equipped to secure a position and be successful as a product marketer. After all, you do have a degree in marketing and did well in your projects and exams. You were a strong contributor in class discussions and class assignments and even demonstrated leadership skills. Well, guess what. The companies who are hiring marketing pros want just that—pros. They go by three tiers: those marketing pros who have worked or who are working for their competitors; the marketing pros who have worked in product marketing outside of their industry but who obviously would have transferable, appropriate skills; and those candidates who have potential to learn and become effective members of their team. That's correct. If you don't have actual work experience, you are in the latter grouping. Your school and your education have provided you with solid potential—nothing else in the real world.

And you thought *Real World* was an old television show, didn't you?

So my point is you want a position within the marketing function so that you can observe, network, learn, and grow in such a way that you can become a product marketer.

Who do you think the department heads will look at first before going to the outside for additional marketing talent? You're there every day, punctual, helpful, learning the company and its processes, and enthusiastically willing to engage in new projects that add to your experience level and to the success of the department and ultimately to the company.

Conversely, if you have long finished with school and have work experience, complete with a track record of achievement, you need to seriously decide on a job or position that you're qualified to do. You're armed with recollections of what you were successful in doing and the jobs where you made significant contributions in performing. You know what you enjoy doing, are good at, and have deep understanding and knowledge of—in short, what you would enjoy doing again! Maybe it's your most recent position with several additional duties, your latest position in a different industry, or the position that you interfaced with on a regular basis and wanted to work in, but there were never any openings in that area. Perhaps you're ready for a management role or a technical leadership role. Maybe you're an engineer with lots of testing experience but little exposure to design and development. Maybe you've been working on the same equipment or software systems and want to broaden your skill set and learn something new. If you're a hotshot programmer, you might want to work with a software language that is more powerful than what you have been working with and know to be limiting. If you're a talented accounting person, could it be that you're tired of keeping track of accounts receivables and payables and would like to move into the role of financial analyst so you can use more of your analytical and forecasting skills? After all, one can only take so much of those long, hectic hours associated with month-end, quarterly, and year-end closes!

Are you now ready for your former supervisor's position or that next position you were slated for before the grim reaper of layoffs darkened the door of your office, entered your cubicle, or summoned you to your boss's office and gave you the bad news? Whatever it is, it must be clear to you. You should know the ins and outs, the in-betweens, and the yins and yangs of it. (We'll discuss more about those later on.)

Simple recap: Treat your job search as the important function it is. Put in the necessary time and effort upfront so that you will be successful. Do not leave your future to chance.

Okay, Sparky, you are now ready to start putting all of that good stuff on paper and develop your résumé.

Chapter 5

DEVELOPING YOUR RÉSUMÉ OR "TO THY OWN SELF BE TRUE"

There are firms that specialize in creating résumés for anyone, and there are outplacement firms who provide résumé writing as part of their service package. Employers (companies) purchase their services after deciding to have a layoff or an RIF (reduction in force). It is as humane an act as they offer after turning your world upside down by laying you off. Usually, it comes as a surprise, although you may have heard rumors circulating about projected downturns in sales or whatever business you may be in, but you were too busy working to pay much attention to rumors. Ready or not, you know that you will need to develop or update your résumé to use in your next job search. You can certainly choose to have a total stranger generate your calling card, your self introduction to the world of career opportunities, and trust that since they are professionals "at that sort of thing" they know best. Or you can trust your instincts and your intimate knowledge of yourself—coupled with a bit of reading and research about what other experts say should be in your résumé.

Think about it. As one of my closest friends and staffing specialist colleagues, James Ratliff, reminded me, "You know what makes you unique." The intangible qualities that only you possess—the way you approach difficult tasks, your coolness under pressure, the way you make those around you perform better (and often better than they thought they could) the languages you speak, along with your functional knowledge of other cultures—all make you the unique you that you are!

There are several popular résumé formats that are prevalent: the reverse chronological, the expanded summary with dates and company listings on the second page, and the combination summary and achievements with no dates or companies listed.

As you may have guessed, the reverse chronological is the most popular and arguably the most effective. It typically has an objective so that the person reading it doesn't have to guess what it is you are applying for or are interested in doing.

The general rule in education placement is that any degree above an undergrad degree goes right after the objective. But if only an undergrad or below, it goes after the experience and above the listing of your training or affiliations. It is also appropriate to combine both education and training, especially if they are related.

Next, it should have a summary or a synopsis section, which describes in general what you've done and the areas of expertise or concentration you've had. It typically mentions some of your professional attributes and may even mention your self-motivation.

It will next have a key accomplishments or accomplishments section, where several of your key accomplishments are stated that are relevant to the objective that you stated at the beginning. A couple of the accomplishments briefly mentioned here should be mentioned in more detail in the body or in the experience section.

The experience section follows, which is the body of your résumé and the second-most important part. It will consist of a detailed, but not in an overly stated manner, your title, your main responsibilities, and several of the challenging aspects encountered that you were able to overcome—including several key accomplishments that reflect your objective and support your accomplishments that are relevant to the job. A well-written résumé tells a succinct yet progressive story instead of writing a laundry list number of responsibilities with nothing about how you performed (i.e., "exceeded sales quota four years in a row" or "as a result of increasing our turnaround time to only twenty-four hours was promoted to technical support supervisor"). There are many ways we contribute to our jobs that we sometimes forget because it becomes routine. If the opposite were true, and there were a series of failures or instances of dropping the ball, as it were, they would not be viewed as routine. Just remember that. (The shortcoming of most résumés is that they read like a series of job descriptions and responsibilities. They don't indicate how well someone did in the execution of those duties and responsibilities. Believe me: employers already know the job functions. They're looking for someone who has been successful in executing them!)

This format (reverse chronological) displays your continuity and can reveal gaps and short durations in employment at several companies. If you were a victim of a companywide, divisionwide, or departmental layoff, state it at the end of the paragraph of those companies. For example, "Due to company layoff, was let go in March 2013." Another example could be "Company relocated our function out of country." (The more you can eliminate questions or misinterpretations about your work ethic or stability in a job, the better.)

One of the prominent advantages in using this format is that it affords you the opportunity to demonstrate your career development and showcase your expertise by succinctly stating your successes, especially those that directly benefited the company. Here are examples:

> As a result of my team's efforts, the company reduced its overruns with an annual savings of $5,000,000.

> By working long hours and weekends, was able to debug a major ASIC design issue, which enabled us to ship the product on time. It saved the company twenty million dollars in orders and preserved our market share for our most advanced product.

> After my team and I developed and implemented a plantwide, cross-training program for everyone's job, we reduced turnover in the last six months from 35 percent to 5 percent and increased productivity by 40 percent.

Now when someone is on vacation or out sick, there is no drop-off in getting the work done on schedule.

Specific examples are well received and are indicators of past impressive results to the bottom line, something all companies relate to. But more importantly, they are indicators of potential successes for your future employer.

Caution: As tempting as it may appear, do not, under any circumstances, lay false claim to some blockbusting achievement that you had no hand in producing. It is better to be thought capable of making significant contributions than to claim to have done so falsely. You would be surprised at the number of people who turn up in your career—over and over again. During my career working in several different industries and a host of disciplines, I've worked with some of the same people at two or three different companies! And to give you a little insight into our profession—staffing/headhunting/talent acquisition/human resources—we make our living on information. We do both overt and covert reference checking. Sure, we usually call the references you list on an application or give to us, but we often know someone who worked at the same company during your time there or a professor in your engineering, mathematics, history, sociology, or English department—or whatever your main course of study—when you were doing your final project for your undergrad degree all the way up to your postdoctoral projects. We aren't necessarily looking for negative information. We're looking for areas that motivate you, what you're passionate about, what you excel at, your consistency and reliability, and/or your demonstrated teamwork or leadership capabilities, depending on the requirements of the position or the growth of the company.

When it comes to recruiting highly sought-after talent, some of my colleagues almost never turn it off. An introduction or a casual chat turns into a mini-interview—at concerts, wedding receptions, memorial services, waiting on line at the market, a coffee shop, or the movies—just about any place where people gather and have a few minutes to talk. (When I started in the placement/hiring/staffing business back in the mid 1970s, I would interview everyone I came in contact with. My since-departed wife at the time, Charlotte, who was quite supportive usually, one evening had had enough. She gave me a gentle elbow to my arm and reminded me that I was not at work but at a social event. She whispered emphatically, "So just make conversation and stop interviewing everybody!" Naturally, she was right, so I complied. From that day forward, I promised myself that I would always carry a small stack of business cards to give to those people I would have most likely been interviewing previously. <Grin>

The more information we have, the better our chances of making a good hire.

We may meet that "good hire" anywhere, and they may not even be looking for a job or they may want to but haven't decided when or how to begin the process just yet. We typically refer to these *potential* candidates as "passive candidates" who will need some encouraging and assistance in making steps to pursue a better opportunity—or at least our opportunity, the one we have in mind for them. We may contact them via a website after doing a search for their particular skill set. We may approach them at a convention, conference, or some professional meeting where they spoke, presented a paper, or manned a booth at a career fair.

Good hires stay and grow with the company. They usually find the job they want in the type of work environment they enjoy, and in addition to an acceptable wage, salary, or compensation package, the distance that they have to travel to get there is doable for them. In places where there is limited public transportation and the jobs are long distances away from where people are employed, commuting can be a challenge. I know of friends and former colleagues who still get up at "zero dark thirty" in order to beat the morning traffic to get to work on time. I once had a contract technical recruiter assignment that was about sixty miles away, but because of the traffic in both the morning and evening, my commute took about an hour and twenty-five minutes each way on a good day. If there was a delay due to an auto accident or a motorcycle losing a battle with a truck that turned too sharply, my commute could take up to two and a half hours! One of the many amazing things about living in the Bay Area of northern California is that most geographic regions have their own distinct microclimates. So on my way to work, I would pass through three or four of them, each a little warmer than the last since I was headed south toward, but a considerable distance from, Los Angeles. Anyway, by the time I arrived at work, I was quite overdressed for the temperature there. Since it was cool where I lived and started from, I would be wearing a sweater with a jacket or a jacket with a long-sleeved shirt, only to see my fellow employees wearing short sleeves and some in T-shirts and other summery clothes stare at me as though I had come from some foreign land or another planet! I worked there over a year before transferring to a location closer to home. But long before that, I had adjusted to the time on the road (I listened to audio books and lots of good music!) and even to the temperature difference that I likened to working in Florida without the humidity!

So it certainly helps to take the necessary steps to find the job that is truly right for you. This means what you are good at doing, what you really want to do, and where you will go to do the job! We often hear that if you have a passion for doing something, it doesn't seem like work. Well, I believe that passion is born out of curiosity that becomes enthusiastic interest and a burning desire to be successful pursuing that interest. Each requires action, so go toward that job that you are curious about, interested in, and apply your total self to reach success!

Another thing worth mentioning about good hires is that they usually get promoted and may become hiring managers for us to work with again. At that time, however, they are on the *other* side of the desk, asking pertinent questions while conducting interviews themselves.

A final point about our process in identifying good candidates is that while we are gathering information to determine good hires, should we turn up negative information of dishonesty, a reputation of being difficult to work with, or discover fabricated claims of accomplishments, we most likely will eliminate that candidate posthaste! Now let's move along. Just remember the reverse chronological format should be used when you can do so.

(Check out the following examples of a Reverse Chronological format, including a recent grad applicant.)

Calio Humtdun

1 South Pinnacle Ave.
Savannah Shores, GA 23145

Tel: 527.319.6702   **Email:** crabhuntpier.net

Objective: To obtain a position as an administrative assistant in an environment that offers growth and stability.

Summary: A committed and conscientious professional who is detailed oriented with excellent follow-through. Has a sense of urgency for priorities and short deadline projects. Effective communicator and computer literate with the ability and willingness to teach others. Well organized and learns systems and procedures quickly and easily. Proficient in MS Office Suite, Internet search, appointment scheduling, and creating and maintaining easy to use filing systems.

Experience:

Miller Highlife Hospital, Allergy Div. Mildew, MD. June 2012–July 2015

Administrative Assistant

- Scheduled meetings and maintained the activity calendars for three managers.
- Coordinated in-house workshops and seminars.
- Was responsible for data entry and checking for accuracy.
- Maintained sensitive and confidential information and financial reports.
- Created monthly activity reports for the three managers and performed special projects when needed.
- Successfully reorganized a broken, ineffective customer support tracking system that saved the hospital over $130,000. (Position ended because the Allergy Division was sold to Itchi Pharmaceuticals in Pakistan and 98 percent of employees were laid off.)

41

Education:

Kenneigan Valley College North Sandwich, MI. April 2012

- Certificate of completion in IT, MS Office Suites, business theory, ten-key data entry, computer theory, Basic and Visual Basic programming
- Received the honor student of the semester award
- Graduated high school magna cum laude

Other Interests and Activities:

- Member, Tutors for a Better Tomorrow
- Chairperson, Sewing Circle for Future Leaders
- Kenneigan Alumni, Lifetime Membership

Franklin R. Shimout

45 Sandy Beach Cove, St. Walter Parrish, Bermuda 07032. Tel: 02.541.8907. Email: musselsrhot.net.

Objective:
A medical assistant position in a clinic or hospital.

Summary:
Highly motivated recent grad with a burning desire to work in the medical field using my education and thirst for medical knowledge in helping others. Very cooperative and willing to work long, arduous hours to learn and develop into a strong, reliable contributor to the team. Has a penchant for remembering names and very minute details and processes. Computer savvy and enjoys research in a laboratory setting. Solid knowledge of anatomy, trained in first aid and CPR. Very familiar with medical terminology, medical ethics, and confidentiality.

Education and Externships:
AS degree, Medical Care and Research College of Health, St. Croix, WI, June 2015. X-ray technician extern, Healing Hospital, Eastern Michigan, IN, Feb 2015. Patient care extern, Mercy Healing Labs, Southgate, VA, June 2014.

Other Activities and Interests:
Tutor math to high school students at Jack Robinson Community College (summer job); Teach English to ESL adult students at Jack Robinson Community College (summer job); Self-taught alto saxophone player; member, Medicos of Tomorrow.

Certifications:
Medical assistant (with distinction), Feb 2012. Medical terminology, Feb 2012. CPR/AED workshop, May 2013. X-ray assistant, Feb 2014.

Soolarri Yenkens

1234 Babbling Brook Lane
Cochise, Maryland 43521
Sunrise44.jenkins@pnctglobal.com

Objective
Senior-level recruiter or employment manager using my twenty-plus years of high-tech, generalist recruiting, and management experience to achieve high-volume, time-critical, staffing objectives.

Education
MS, advanced thinking, University of Okinawa, Naha, Okinawa
Concentration in qualitative and quantitative analysis

Professional Training: Behavioral interviewing workshops, legal aspects of hiring; Resumix, Restrac, Personic, Virtual Edge, Icarian, and Taleo Applicant Tracking Systems' training; legal aspects of human resources, including confidentiality, sexual harassment, and job performance/

evaluation and proper dismissals within the law. Internet sourcing proficiency and full-cycle recruiting.

Summary

- A senior-level recruiter with over twenty years of high-technology hiring experience in a variety of industries and disciplines.
- Effective in streamlining hiring and human resources systems and procedures that have resulted in time and money savings.
- An effective manager who enjoys the challenge and successes of managing senior-level and junior-level staffing personnel alike.
- A conscientious staffing professional with a sense of urgency in filling hard-to-fill, critical openings.

Key Accomplishments

- Staffed up a start-up operation in less than ninety days that was critical to the life of the company's investment and long-term technology objectives.
- Developed and conducted informal and formal training sessions for hiring supervisors and managers within the operations area of a high-tech manufacturing company.
- Consistently among the top three producers within the staffing department, both inside companies and while working in employment agencies.
- Through hard work and persistence, motivated indifferent-seeming hiring managers to cooperate and allocate weekly focused time for staffing activities. We were successful in the timely filling of forty critical openings in less than ninety days.

Experience
Good Outcome and Solutions, Inc. Imagination, OH. June 2017 to Present
Manager, Staffing
For this make-believe company that doesn't really exist, was instrumental in reducing their cost-per-hire and hiring time for their start-up division (Telepathic Phototonics) that has revolutionized the way smart phones,

smart watches, and smart eyeglasses communicate and process data. Hired a staff of six recruiters, two sourcers, and two administrative assistants for this start-up effort and filled more than one hundred openings in less than four months. Developed, implemented, and trained hiring managers on new, more effective hiring procedures.

Currently engaged in hiring process engineers, software engineers, sales and product marketing, analysts, financial analysts, purchasing agents, buyer/planners, cost accountants, program managers, project coordinators, and several IT system developers. Provide training for newly hired and junior-level recruiters.

Clim-Lim Research & Development, Inc. Brainthrust, CA. May 2014 to June 2017
Sr. Staffing Specialist/Program Manager
For this equally imagined research company, I functioned as the staffing program manager for all the openings in its Future Technology Division. This division, which was established to focus on technology products five to six years in the future, required forward, innovative thinking engineers and managers in order for it to be successful. I was able to attract and hire forty-five highly motivated, talented professionals into the software, firmware, technical analysis, hardware, tech support, and product engineering ranks in a six-month period. During slow hiring periods, I assisted my human resources colleagues with reorganization plans, employee evaluations, and bonus program development to include all company employees.

Calmdown Industries, Inc. Sleepy Hollow, FL. Jan 2010 to April 2014
Sr. Recruiter
For this made-up company that only exists in my mind, I was initially assigned to the Sleep Deprivation Division. It was tasked to identify solutions for insomnia, and to later publish its findings to the SDSA (Sleep Disorder Scientific Association). Candidates for this undertaking consisted of sleep researchers, meditators, long-distance truck drivers, and technologists. After six months, the project was shelved due to excessive absenteeism and physical exhaustion. I was reassigned to the Wide Awake Division, which was tasked to develop energy "in a bottle" for commercial

use. Successfully hired a team of thirty enthusiastic, out-of-the-building-thinking research engineers in a month and a half. In addition to the hiring of specialty engineering areas, was responsible for the sales and marketing openings that occurred throughout the company.

Previous Experience
Full-cycle technical recruiter for two start-up companies that developed electronic products for the automobile and the aeronautics industries.

Affiliations and Associations
Member, Society for Responsible Hiring
Member, Society for Corporate Integrity and Equitable Pay

Charlie C. Johnston
13 Longway Around Terrace, St Charles, MN 21345
Charlietoyou@mylife.net
946.615.4433

Objective:
A network administrator position within an IT organization that will utilize my experience and skills to meet/exceed company goals and objectives.

Synopsis:
With ten-plus years in the information technology industry, I have a broad range of experience, including IT project management, desktop technical support, department trainer, as well as developing, testing and implementing business technology solutions. Conceptualized and created timesaving, leading edge, engineering systems that set the standards for the web server environment. I have a solid testing background—in both development and off-the-shelf package implementation. I have been an effective team player and have demonstrated leadership in roles that required sound judgment and project management. I work equally well with end users and technical colleagues, and consistently demonstrate that I am a quick learner with a positive, cooperative attitude.

Experience:

Nonexistent, Inc.   **Heartbreak, WY**   **Dec 2012–Present**
Sr. Systems Administrator

- Analyze, research, and develop solutions for issues and problems on PCs and the network.
- Install, maintain, and support of network applications.
- Analyze, install, and tune SQL Server databases.
- Support the LAN/WAN and Windows Server environment, including enterprise mission critical servers, applications, and network routing.
- Develop and maintain website monitoring services.
- Research and recommend new products for the web server environment.
- Provide technical support regarding web best practices, and incorporate new technologies as needed.

Off the Top Labs, GoFish, MO   **Apr 2009–Oct 2012**
Network/Desktop Support Technician

- More than three years installing, troubleshooting, and connecting PCs and laptops.
- Successfully repaired or replaced disk drives, floppy and CD-ROM drives, zip drives, keyboards, and modems.
- Diagnosed and eliminated various viruses using IBM and Norton antivirus products.
- Provided technology model for business plan and constructed the backbone of the network infrastructure.
- Administered Windows NT network.
- Developed and implemented corporate intranet report site and corporate-wide databases with the use of MS Access
- Responsible for installs and upgrade of hardware and software, system monitoring, capacity planning, installing patches and hot fixes, troubleshooting, and resolved configuration issues.

Northcoast Labs, Inc.   Drought, AR   Sept 2004–Apr 2009
Network Engineer/Test Engineer

- Configured, verified, and troubleshoot Cisco routers.
- Established network security guidelines using Symantec and Nitron products.
- Designed network infrastructure and Windows networking.
- Wrote power supply testing procedures and tested redundancy power supply systems to ensure proper functioning and safety.
- Was responsible for upgrading, converting, troubleshooting, maintaining, and monitoring Windows servers and the corporate-wide network.
- Developed and implemented data backup and recovery policy and procedures.

Trained junior level engineers and tech support staff.

The expanded summary with dates and companies listed format is generally used by candidates who have gaps in their job history or who have short durations at a number of jobs they've had and want to emphasize what they did versus the lack of time spent at those jobs. As such, they have paragraphs describing their abilities, responsibilities, and accomplishments. Naturally, there are many reasons for their gaps or short-term job history. In cases of employment gaps, it could be they had returned to school full-time to obtain a higher-level degree (MBAs are often useful in pursuing business, marketing, or management positions) and are now returning to the workforce. Or perhaps they are applying for a position they held several jobs ago and now want one similar to it without revealing that they've been out of that industry or function for quite some time.

Regarding those with short durations spent at what seemed like good jobs where they made significant contributions, I don't mean to imply that these candidates are less than honest, smart-working professionals. On the contrary, many of these professionals would have continued their career paths if they had the opportunity to do so. More likely, their company relocated, transferred their function (sometimes their whole division or department) overseas, business dropped significantly, their projected sales in the future, say three quarters or so, were dismal so the company was going to have to cut expenses accordingly, or their company was acquired and their role became duplication or excess. Since they had to continue bringing home the turkey bacon and the fresh vegetables and salads for their healthy-eating family, they took jobs that were available—whether along their career path or not.

If there is an advantage with this format, it is that the candidate gets to state upfront and continuously the depth of their capabilities through describing their major achievements, key contributions, and qualifications.

The order of this format is as follows:

Again, the contact information is on the top followed by the objective underneath, and like the reverse chronological format, the education, if it is more than an undergrad, goes under the objective. Next we have the summary section, where you state your professional attributes and abilities. (I've actually seen a professional profile section in addition to the summary section, but that can sometimes be redundant.) Remember these should relate or be associated with your objective, more than likely the behavior and capabilities necessary to perform the job you seek. Here you will see items such as these:

- "meticulous attention to detail"
- "an effective communicator with experience in negotiating labor contracts"
- "capable trainer who has developed curricula for a variety of technical disciplines"
- "extensive experience in designing, developing, real-time embedded systems"
- "productive team player who works well in crisis or with ambitious project deadlines"
- "exceptional quantitative skills"
- "solid financial modeling and cost experience"

I'm sure you get my drift.

Next comes the accomplishments section, or some would call the key or major accomplishments where more detailed information is stated about your background that is relevant to your objective and the job you want. Since you know what the job entails or what skills are being sought, you certainly know which of your significant accomplishments are related to the job. Please don't give a laundry list of your accomplishments without ensuring that they are relevant to the job and expressed in a precise and easy-to-understand manner. You're painting a mental picture that should flow and flow with consistency. A person reading your résumé should know what you want, who you are, and what you've done. There should not be any undue effort on the reader's part to have to go on an expedition throughout your résumé to determine what you want, who you are, or what you've done that relates to the job you are pursuing!

Now for your dates and companies list, headings for these vary, including "Work History," "Work Experience," "Professional Employment," or "Employment." Then go ahead and list them in reverse chronological order with the month and year of starting and the month and year each employment ended. It is perfectly fine to list as your last day on the company's payroll versus the last day worked, because companies will often give an employee some grace time to assist them in looking for another position. This is especially true in cases where there are RIFs or layoffs through no fault of the employee.

221 Marauder Way, Spring Living, WY 32510
Cell: (445) 300-2102
Hannibalsrevenge.rmp@elephant.netts

J.D. Marpier, Jr.
Objective: Financial Management

Education: MBA with majors in international finance and management— University of Malcolm Little (Detroit, MI)

CPA (certified public accountant) University of Atlantis, Barbados, WI

CMA (certified management accountant) University of Kemet, Praise, TX

Summary: An accomplished CFO, director of finance, senior accounting manager, cost accounting manager, and financial consultant for start-up and expanding technology companies. Experienced in all aspects of finance and accounting functions with both international and domestic hands-on responsibility. I have over twenty years' experience of financial/accounting operations, managing multifunctioning areas, and establishing mid- and long-term strategic direction and objectives. Intimately familiar with the complete cost accounting function, including accounting procedures, standard cost, sales, and cost of sales analysis. Possess excellent interpersonal and effective management skills. Broad and deep understanding of the unique challenges in the high-tech sector with a track record of achievement both locally and around the globe.

Key Accomplishments/Contributions

- Participated in and managed the integration of three recently acquired companies (two domestic and one international) into the corporate framework and functions.
- Effectively managed a team of international and domestic accounting, financial analysis, systems migration, cost accounting, and corporate P&L with close working ties to mergers and acquisitions.
- Spearheaded the implementation of critical, more efficient accounting systems (accounts receivable/payable, payroll, and cost accounting) that increased productivity over 35 percent.
- Created the new cost system implementation and conversion team and established the coordinated worldwide standard cost and update procedures.
- Directed the strategic direction and consolidation of all offshore manufacturing and repair sites' operating budgets, forecasts and reporting, resulting in a corporate savings of thirteen million dollars, US.
- Through close working relationships with the banking community, was able to reduce banking fees by 25 percent with a considerable savings of $500,000.

- Directed the analysis and updating of corporate-wide system security and internal audits.
- Provided the leadership and direction to develop an effective, customer-focused, financial service and satisfaction department.

Work History
Scotchgood, Intl. Plymouth, ND
CFO, director of finance Jan 2008–Aug 2013

Micro-DP, Industries, Inc. St. Geronimo, CA
Director of finance, sr. accounting manager Oct 2000–Jan 2008

Park Avenue Industries, Inc. East Orange, NJ
Sr. manager, cost accounting Apr 1992–June 1998

Greensleaves Accounting, Inc. Rochester, NH
Consultant, general accounting June 1990–Apr 1992

Affiliations and Organizations
- International Finance Society, past chair CPA Association of Manufacturing
- Cost Accountants of Toronto

Education:
Sierra Leone Institute, Djembe, Republic of Benin
Major: BS Network Science

Technical Skills:
Languages: Visual Basic, Fox Pro, Basic, C+, C dBase, Html, JAVA, and Assembly
Operating System: UNIX, Linux, Netware, Microsoft NT Windows NT, DNS, and
WINS, IBM AS/400, and Apple OS
Networking: Ethernet 10baseT, Token Ring and Arcnet, TCP/IP

Interests and Organizations:
Member, Olympic Planning Committee

Member, Chiracauwau, AZ Fencing Team
Volunteer, Big Brother Organization of Sedona, AZ

The combination summary and achievements with no dates or companies listed version consists of contact information at the top and a summary and accomplishments section pretty much integrated that describes what this person has done over a period of time and what accomplishments or successes they have had. It is typically used by someone who has not seriously committed to seeking another career opportunity. Their attitude is that if you are interested in this summary, etc. and want to talk with them, they are willing to listen. And with a bit of coaxing, they may even throw something together in the form of a résumé. Give me a break!

It reminds me of the times I would see friends and acquaintances at concerts or other social settings and they would ask, "Did you find me that job yet? I'm really tired of working at so and so." I would remind them that I still needed their résumé for me to keep an eye out for them. To which they would often reply, "Don't worry. I'm working on it, and I'll get it to you before the week is out." Well, dear reader, maybe they sent their masterpiece of a résumé to you, because I sure as heck never received them!

But to be fair, sometimes this style or résumé format is utilized because the candidate was contacted in the past by someone who worked with him before. They were familiar with the candidate's work and could vouch for it but needed something quick to pass along to their boss or "to those HR (human resources) folks" in order to have him scheduled for an interview. Well, this person hasn't had to look for a job before now and since that format did the trick before, they'll use it again. No, no, *noooooooo!* Do not use it for anything more than a reference guide to remind you of pertinent information to include when developing your *real résumé.*

Solari Jenkins

Joanie B. Good, CPA

chuckberrytune@hits.net Cell: 754.213. 6430

Summary and Achievements
An accounting professional with more than fifteen years of broad-based accounting experience that includes general ledger, accounts payable/receivable, payroll, account reconciliation, internal auditing, and financial reporting.

Responsible for all aspects of A/P and A/R and wrote off $350,000 worth of accounts receivables. Maintained payroll for four hundred employees. Analyzed and instituted systems to implement seamless, integrated accounting processes. Supervised, coordinated, and analyzed cross-charging activities between corporate and its five divisions. Implemented automation tools that reduced processing time by 38 percent. Implemented accounting procedures for month-end and year-end close that significantly reduced overtime and long hours. Supervised accountants during audits and audit reports for multiple divisions. Reviewed and evaluated accounting systems, internal controls, and operating procedures; our recommendations were accepted and implemented. Financial accounting and reporting process analysis and redesign. Worked closely with the IT department to automate and make available online general ledger, work order, and trial balance reports that the three unit managers could access twenty-four/seven, that saved the corporation approximately thirty hours a month. Responsible for credit limit process implementation and credit qualifying of new customers for all regional markets. Dramatically increased the time and accuracy of collection activity. Secured short- and long-term bank financing for expansion efforts.

Education

CPA
Dragon Tail University
San Mateo, CA
BS degree in accounting and finance
Cloisonne College
Bangkok, Thailand

54

Now, before we move on, let's deal with continuity and the things that generally raise red flags and cause candidates *not to be* contacted.

When a staffing person or a hiring manager looks at a résumé, they are looking for certain things. If there is an objective, it should reflect the summary/ qualifications and accomplishments, with the experience section giving more detail. You would be surprised at how many résumés were disqualified because the résumé's objective stated that they wanted something different than what the job was listed as. For example, the objective stated that the person wanted a position as manager, when the job was not a manager but an individual contributor with no managerial responsibility.

As we would read further, there were several references to having managed a diverse group of people and achieving outstanding successes—while completing impressive-sounding projects on time and under budget. The problem was the position they were applying to was not a manager job! I think some people believe that if they can show that they performed at a higher level, then it follows that they could surely do a lower-level position that may have even reported to them!

Au contraire, my industrious, bright friend. Although some managers have hands-on experience and knowledge, there are areas they simply have no experience in doing except during their days in college while trying to pass a class. For example, equipment and maintenance technicians have a craft that few engineers possess, although they work closely together. The engineers usually have high-level technicians run their experiments or tests on the machines that the equipment and maintenance technicians install, test, repair, and maintain. So a manager of engineering who had engineers and technicians reporting to them seldom had opportunities to develop those skills and would not be the best candidate to bring onboard in that capacity. Also, we should not think that various levels of company employees are better than others just because of their lofty titles. I remember how I fought against referring to individual-contributor employees as "employees" while those in managerial positions were referred to as "management." (How silly this was, I thought, since we were all employees of the company regardless of our titles!)

As we give more detail in our experience section, if you are seeking a programmer analyst or software engineer position, for example, some reference to programming and software development should be in those two areas, and it should be prominent and easily recognized. Remember you are not applying for a class or a workshop or volunteering for some public service organization. You are applying for a job, and you have something to offer: skills, experience, and past successes. So state them!

I once met a candidate who was tired of waiting for his career to take off as quickly as he thought it should, so he put his résumé together and started making the rounds at job fairs. (Yes, job fairs were very popular before the advent of the Internet with its search engines and job boards!) When he approached the booth of the high-tech company where I worked at the time as its staffing manager, he was dressed in a nice-looking, business suit, starched shirt, and tie. He was well groomed, complete with shined shoes that completed his professional appearance.

After we exchanged greetings and introductions, I asked what he was interested in doing for us. He said he wanted to apply for the manager of procurement position that we had listed in our three pages of openings at the time. "Fine," I said. "Let's see your résumé."

He reached into his case and handed me his résumé. Well, I quickly scanned it, noticing his qualifications section, his experience, his schooling, and even his hobbies, but I couldn't find anything to do with procurement or purchasing anywhere on it! So I asked him, "Where is your procurement experience?"

He calmly answered, "I don't have any, but I interface with them on a regular basis and I know what they do. They will train here, right?"

"Uh no, they won't train," I said while trying not to display my disappointment that he had no experience in a position that was critical for us at the time. As I further studied his résumé, I asked him what was so attractive about a position that he had no experience in doing. He mentioned that he had been promised he would have opportunities leading into management with his current employer, yet none had come in the three years he had worked there. He thought it was time to move on, and since he felt this was a good company and he knew *something* about the function of procurement, he'd give it a shot.

Well, my dear page-turning friend, I thought this a perfect time to offer some career counseling. After asking about his relationship and communication frequency with his boss, what he really felt about his present company/employer—his likes and dislikes, etc.—I suggested that he set up a meeting with his boss away from their work place, on neutral ground, say over lunch at a quiet restaurant not far from their offices. He was to bring his last evaluation or annual review, a list of his most productive or most successful projects, and a description of what he wanted to be considered for going forward.

Sometimes we don't get noticed for promotions or expanded responsibilities until we make it known that we are ready for advancement. (Yes, I know. One-on-one meetings with your supervisor, manager, or boss are times to make such desires known, but too many times those meetings are used for updating your boss on your progress on the projects you're working on. They will want to discuss what issues you may have encountered that might jeopardize you completing them on time. Those discussions get so involved that there is hardly time for much else.) Well, let's call my ambitious friend Adam. I don't know if he ever got what he wanted, but I never saw him again at any of the job fairs that I attended. I hope he went back and approached his career like a pro and not one who bails before doing due diligence to ensure a career path of more responsibility, growth, and promotion.

Another turnoff is for a résumé to go on and on about how wonderful you are and how effective you've been in a number of areas, but have no objective stating what you want to do now. To compound the mystery, the experience section has a variety of positions listed that are all over the map. These talented professionals, who have demonstrated adaptability in a variety of positions, often have their résumés put aside because no one wants to guess what they are interested in pursuing at this point. And we cannot assume, because sometimes people want to do something different from what they've been doing. (Yes, we've heard the argument, mostly from outplacement firms, the companies that make their living on company layoffs or downsizing by counseling the laid-off employees on résumé preparation (but will also create one for you if needed), career coaching, and by sharing helpful tips and information to overcome the impact of being laid-off and being out of work. Well, I've heard their counselors say that you don't need an objective on your résumé. They suggest that you prepare a cover letter that is tailored to the particular position you want and that is sufficient.

Also, I've observed that certain government positions and those in the academic community often request a cover letter. I'll let you in on a little secret. There are many staffing professionals/recruiters, those who work in talent acquisition, and hiring managers who never bother to read cover letters! They've found too many times that a cover letter will talk about what the job seeker wants, but there is no mention of ever having done what the cover letter states they want to do in their experience! So you can do a bit of research to see which is most effective in getting someone to contact you, but I would lean toward the people who are involved in hiring on a daily basis—from the inside.

Let's not forget that a number of companies have an automated system or an ATS (Applicant Tracking System) that screens résumés electronically while also keeping track of each candidate who applies to any position. These in-house systems track from the application all the way through the process of getting interviewed, hired, or rejected. Be sure, whenever possible, to include some of the key words or phrases mentioned in the job description qualifications. That way, the system will read them on your résumé and will include rather than exclude you on its initial screening. This also helps the staffing people as well, since there are instances when a technical requirement is so specialized that it is good to clearly state that you have that particular skill set or experience. It could make a huge difference.

Résumés that stand out from the crowd and thus have *you* stand out are the ones that use action words (e.g., augmented, collected, designed, detected, expedited, identified, established, produced, created, prioritized, investigated, researched, and reinforced). A résumé that only states your responsibilities without any successes is boring and labels you a card-carrying member of the masses. However, if you put forth the effort to mention the challenges you faced on a particular project and what you did to tackle it, the skills acquired, the other groups or departments you involved in resolving the challenges, and the ultimate outcome (if you can do this for each of the jobs you've had), your résumé will breathe with life. It will be a true reflection of your competence and of what you've accomplished. Compared to the many others, yours will definitely stand out and become (almost) exciting reading.

Finally, let's remember to be informative yet succinct. We can make a solid case why we should get the nod without writing a *War and Peace* epic. And for you management-level candidates, be careful of using too much of the pronoun *I* in your successes. Put more of "we," "my team," and "our department." Seldom does a hiring manager or staffing person look favorably upon a manager who takes all the credit for his group's successes. Plus it will raise a flag about one of your most critical responsibilities as a manager: whether you helped develop your direct reports and your ability to make good hires!

Let's summarize what we've covered. We recognize that our résumé is our calling card, and when done properly and honestly, it will serve us well as a proper representative or agent in our quest for securing the job we want. We will spend the appropriate time to ensure that it is a true reflection of our experience, skills acquired and utilized, our contributions, and our successes. We will use the proper format, and we will have the objective, qualifications or summary, accomplishments, and experience sections all relate to what we are looking to do in our next position. Action words will be utilized to demonstrate a can-do, have-done, and still-capable-of personality and work ethic. We will use good judgment in how much detail we go into, while being ever mindful that "A word to the wise is sufficient." And should an employer request a cover letter, we will develop one that speaks to our background and the job we are pursuing.

Chapter 6

INTERVIEWS CAN BE FUN (ALMOST) WHEN YOU ARE PROPERLY PREPARED

Most of the established corporations, and certainly most of the corporations that have an HR (human resources) department, will conduct behavioral and situational interviews. It's one thing to ask how you would respond to a given situation, but it is more telling to have you recall how you responded to a situation that you actually experienced. Seldom do candidates have a number of interviewers say, "Tell me about yourself," without following up with several behavioral or situational questions. Companies want to know how you set your goals, how you interface with others, within your team and with other departments, how flexible you are, how driven you are, if you can accept criticism without becoming defensive and emotional, if you can be relied upon once you give your word, and how committed are you to becoming the best you can be.

On the other hand, if you are asked to tell them about yourself, but with no follow-up question or nothing that would steer the conversation into a discussion relevant to the position you're interviewing for, then you are talking with an amateur who knows very little about interviewing! Unfortunately, they exist in too many company settings. In those cases, you will have to pretty much guide the interview in the direction of the job and answer questions relevant to it.

Previously, I mentioned some of the reasons applicants give for seeking a new career opportunity. Picture yourself in an interview and the question comes up "Why are you interested in pursuing another job at this time?" After giving your answer, a follow-up question could be "What are you looking to gain in a new job that isn't available to you currently?" This gives you an opportunity to answer the question, but to also promote yourself. As part of the answer, you insert that you have since "gained knowledge in (blank)," ideally something relevant to the position you're interviewing for, while also increasing your knowledge in (blank) another aspect of the job you're interviewing for.

Other questions that are usually asked are about getting along well with others. We know that there are a lot of hard-charging, driven-toward-excellence, "I'm on my way to the top," go-getter professionals out there. Believe it or not, many people work in their dream job and would do nothing else. I once heard of a software engineer who won the lottery for millions of dollars. After collecting his money, he invested some and put the rest in the bank, bought himself a new car, a couple of new T-shirts, and returned to work as though nothing life-changing had occurred. He obviously was doing exactly what he wanted with his life! Believe me: these professionals take what they do very seriously and sometimes will seem brusque and impatient with people or things that impede their workflow.

Common questions around resolving conflict or disagreements usually sound like "Can you give an example of a work-related conflict or disagreement that occurred between you and another employee, what happened, and how you resolved it?" It's a fair question about your interacting—some might even say your coping skills—so you should have an example. Again, this is an opportunity to answer with a specific example while adding a little something about you as a professional who realizes that it's business and not personal.

Remember this is not one of those "Run tell the boss/supervisor/manager cases." No manager wants to be called into every conflict when the two professionals should be able to work out a solution. As I like to say when discussing this topic during an interview, "The resolution of a problem doesn't start after the problem has occurred. The resolution started before there was a problem." I mean, when you are a true team player and professional who acknowledges others with a greeting in the hallways, lends a hand when needed regardless of whether the person is on your team or not, and generally extends professional courtesies on a consistent basis, you've created good will and demonstrated an approachable, professional personality. Later, having a disagreement with someone you are familiar with makes getting to a resolution much easier than if you two were total strangers.

Conflicts vary and can be about a host of things. In manufacturing, research, or testing environments, they can consist of two technicians, test engineers, or research analysts needing to use the same test equipment at the same time. Given the rapid rate of change and expansion of technology, this is a routine occurrence, since each one is trying to complete their tasks by their ambitious deadlines.

Other problem questions are about people you work with directly and the question may be "Share an example of a situation where one of your team members disagreed with you on your proposal, analysis, or solution regarding a critical project or activity, what you did, and what the outcome was." It stands to reason that we will be challenged from time to time within our peer group, but your reaction to those challenges will demonstrate your professional mind-set and how you work within a team. In some professions, this could be a conflict around scheduling, say scheduling time for bus runs or time to complete certain tasks like deliveries or pickups. Deal with these differences in a thoughtful, nondefensive, noncombative, manner, but do voice your opinion supported by facts.

When it comes to flexibility and adaptability, many questions and situations come to mind, but most are common sense responses, such as to continue being productive despite possible changes. How you respond to unexpected changes in direction, priorities, and even layoffs or other critical occurrences says a lot about you and your professionalism. Here are a few to ponder over: "Tell me about a situation where you had to readjust your goals or work schedule due to internal changes. What challenges did it create for you? What did you do to make the adjustment?"

Another one often used to gauge your flexibility is "Tell me about a time when you had to take an unpopular stance on a position and what would have convinced you to change your mind. Have there been times when you gave in? What were the circumstances?" Or simply "After you've analyzed something, tested it, and drawn a conclusion, what does it take for you to change your position?" "In the past two years, what has prevented you from being as successful as you would have liked? What role has management played in your success, and in your frustration? What type of manager have you been most successful, what type the least, and why?"

Interviewers want to know things from your past that might occur while working for them, so they might ask questions like "You mentioned that you left your job at (blank) because it was no longer challenging and didn't offer you career growth. After being in your current job for three years, have you realized the goals you had when you made the move? If yes, please give examples. If not, why not?" Companies want to know if you are a serial job hopper, someone who just hasn't found the right environment for your passion, or what might make you happy and become a long-term employee.

In the area of success or accomplishments that you stated in your summary or qualifications section on your résumé, be prepared to answer detailed questions about several of them. Questions starting with "What job-related (or in cases of recent college grads, what school-related) accomplishment are you most proud of, and why?" usually are followed up with "What did you learn from that experience?"

Now this would be a good time to get to some job-specific questions (i.e., "What part of this job do you foresee being the most challenging, and what will be the least challenging, and why?").

In the case of going into an area that you haven't worked in before or a management role where you've only been a project lead or program manager but not a manager of people and projects or programs, a fair question to begin that topic is "Why do you feel that you are qualified for this job, and how would you go about being successful in doing it?"

Whatever reason you give, be prepared to give relevant examples of what you've done in the past that corroborates your claim. You may encounter an interviewer who is short on words but wants solid, well-thought-out responses (i.e., "Why do you want this job" or "Why should we hire you?"). Again, do not respond with short, half-baked answers. I've seen applicants give cute, almost comedic answers to this manner of questioning, thinking it was sort of a joke and not taking the interview seriously. Although the interviewer may have smiled or chuckled over the response, you were already being relegated to the "No further action" status.

As for management-level interviews, the questions include what you've done to demonstrate your management of people, how you affected your team/department's success, their growth, resolving conflict, and goal setting, just to name some of the key areas of interest. Some of the common questions include the following:

- During the last twenty-four months, please describe tough decisions you made to improve the effectiveness of your organization.
- What would have been the consequences if you hadn't, and how has it changed your organization?
- Please describe your approach or system in assisting your people achieve their career goals, where have you successfully implemented it, and how.
- Describe a time when you had to convince your boss about something that they were against. What did you do, and what was the outcome?
- What is your most regrettable business-related decision or action, and what did you learn from that experience?
- How do you set goals for yourself, your organization, and how has it changed from when you first began doing so?
- What do you enjoy most about managing, and what do you find most challenging?
- Please describe a situation where you had to solve a conflict between two of your direct reports or between your organization and another, and what was put in place to prevent future occurrences.

In environments that tend to change "marching orders" with some frequency due to changes in business or in their industry, managers sometimes have to give unpopular directives. Here is an example: "Describe a time when you have had to have your organization shift their focus or direction because of a directive you received from your executive team or boss and what action you took to maintain morale, if any."

Let's be certain to cover examples of collaboration, since we know that ranks up there as one of the foremost inner-workings of a coordinated, successful environment. A few questions in that vein might be these:

Describe how you have worked collaboratively within your organization, and with others.

How important has collaboration been in your overall success, and why?

Describe a time when you had to work collaboratively with someone who you didn't especially like or who didn't like you. What has to be in place for a successful collaborative effort, and why?

Okay, I think you get the message; these are questions that reveal how you have functioned (behaved) as a manager. You might want to read them over a few times and start preparing responses based on your experience. The more insight into your past decision-making, responding to surprises, and dealing with normal, everyday occurrences that managers face routinely will give the interviewer reasons to look favorably upon your candidacy. Or not.

As a manager, you are expected to be a leader, while understanding that your productivity and the productivity of your organization need to contribute toward the goals of the company. Therefore, there will be decisions made that you may not agree with, or new processes you may not want to implement, but that is the nature of business and why having an open mind and being flexible and adaptable are very important to being successful.

A Quick Recap

Dig into your memory and mentally relive a variety of business- or project-related occurrences that are representative of what kind of employee or project team member you are or were.

Develop tough questions around your background and experience, questions that could most likely be asked of you depending on your education, background, or experience. Practice your answers and be open to follow-up, probing questions to your answers.

Know your answers inside and out!

Part 3

Chapter 7

COMMON MISTAKES CANDIDATES MAKE

Regarding Résumés

Using what we term as "fluff" for an objective. For example, "A career opportunity with a growing company where I can be a contributing team member and help the company reach its goals." What the heck does that say about the type of job you want? Nothing! Be clear about what you want. A better example is this: "A recruiter coordinator position where computer skills, human resources knowledge, and customer service skills will be effectively utilized." Or something as straightforward as "A management position in inside sales or business development."

Being too brief or sketchy in the text and not giving enough information. I've seen too many times to count the experience section of the résumé having a number of duties listed, which sound very much like what the person's job description looks like. Please invest some time to tell a brief story about your work experience. Your résumé needs to reflect you, the person, and not some job description that you copied and passed off as your experience. It's what you did and how that's important, not some regurgitation of your job descriptions without any indication of your level of success or contribution you made while executing those duties!

Being verbose and going into too much detail, leaving nothing to discuss over an interview.

Not proofreading the finished product objectively and ignoring spelling or grammatical mistakes. Also not checking to see if the dates are accurate or conflict with what you state. (It's difficult to have had two full-time regular jobs at the same period while living in two different states.)

Making false claims about your involvement while working on a particular project, claiming to have expertise in areas that you only have familiarity, and lying about something you did, including completing an educational degree. (Typically, companies do background checks and will discover such lies and will have second thoughts about hiring you. They will think, *If he or she lied about that, what else has he or she, or will he or she lie about?*)

The Telephone Screening or Phone Interview

Please understand that the phone screen is the first interview, so be prepared to answer questions as if you were in a face-to-face interview. Regardless of how casual the person sounds who's asking the questions—or in some cases, matter-of-fact and dry they sound—you answer the questions as completely and as pleasantly as you can. This is not a time to negotiate salary, but if asked about your salary desires, tell them what you are or were making. They are going to find out anyway because they will require a pay stub or some proof of salary from you later on. Don't forget to use this opportunity to get more information about the job: urgency to hire, why it is available, established department or new department, new project, etc.

Be sure to get name and contact information from the person who calls because you need to have that to follow up with them, should you not hear anything in a couple of weeks or more. Sometimes, an internal candidate has turned up and taken the attention away from candidates outside the company. You need to know this so you can continue your search with the same enthusiasm you had prior to the initial phone call.

When Arriving for the Interview

If you see that you'll be late for the interview, call to let someone know. Do not show up late and think that all is well. When you are late, you throw the schedule off and show disrespect for the time of others.

Be courteous to all you meet: in the lobby when you sign-in and to the person who comes to escort you to the interview. There have been instances where the candidate was so rude to the lobby personnel or to the department administrator who came to escort them to the conference room for the interview that when the hiring manager learned about it, she eliminated the candidate from consideration! Remember, these folks work together every day and become like family.

I'm reminded of a story I heard when I first got into the placement business (another name for headhunting) some years ago. It seems that this candidate was in such a rush to get to the interview that he drove too fast and rather recklessly on his way to a morning interview with a Fortune 500 company. Well, in so doing, he cut off several cars when changing lanes and even flashed "the bird" to a couple of his fellow drivers headed to work. As he parked and checked his appearance, grabbed his briefcase with extra résumés and a small portfolio of some of his work, he arrived at the lobby and signed in at the front desk. He was later escorted to the conference room to begin the interview, and after accepting a glass of water, he waited impatiently for it to begin.

Yup, you guessed it! The very first person on the interview schedule, and who walked into the room, was none other than one of the drivers he had cut off and given the finger to! As the story goes, he didn't have a long interview, and he did not get the job.

Heck, I've had company receptionists tell *me* that a candidate was very rude each time they called and also when they came in for a person-to-person interview. Occasionally, a receptionist would pull me aside and say, "I sure hope you don't hire him or her, because they wouldn't do well here." More times than not, they were correct, because receptionists usually work at the same company for years and know nearly everyone, especially the successful employees who have progressed into senior management positions.

During the Interview

Don't be a candidate who has body odor or bad breath. Always check yourself before you leave home, the hotel, or wherever you left from to make the interview. If you are a coffee drinker, you know coffee will leave your breath less than fresh smelling, so always keep a small bottle of breath spray, chewing gum, or breath mints with you at all times. And do not think it is okay to wear a wrinkled shirt as long as you put a tie on it, because it is not! It shows either carelessness on your part or someone who doesn't complete things all the way.

Maintain eye contact with the person or persons conducting the interview. The opposite behavior signals disinterest, lack of confidence, or arrogance. None of those will get you closer to landing the job. I was shy for many years and finally realized that being shy got me nowhere. Be shy outside of work, but get involved, speak up, and present your best self possible in attitude, and in communicating. And for those of you who have cultural differences regarding eye contact, get over it! You can continue your cultural habits outside of work.

Don't respond to a question with a partial answer and then ramble on about something unrelated. Answer the question completely, and if you need to preface your answer first, do so, but quickly get back to the question and your answer to it.

Tell the interviewer things about the company to show that you have done your research on it, but don't follow up with questions about why so and so left, and is so and so really as difficult to work with as you had heard? Red lights begin flashing wildly in the interviewer's head. You are saying you are a gossip and will most likely be a distraction rather than a contributing member of the team.

Use your professional manners. Whenever an interviewer gets up to leave, you get up also. The next person will come in and you should be up to greet them and extend a professional handshake. Ladies, this goes for you as well. This is business, not social.

Don't badmouth a former employer or boss. Most people realize that all environments are not perfect fits for everyone, but don't badmouth, no matter how tempting it is to do so. There are many appropriate ways to handle a bad situation. "There have been no promotions in my department for four years and the prospects of me getting promoted are very slim." Or you might want to say, "I've gone as far as I can in my present company. Since it is a small, privately owned company, advancement and broadening my skills are limited." One more that comes to mind would be "The company is going in a different direction from where I want my career to go."

Don't finish the sentence of the interviewer who is talking. I'm not sure if this is a sign of nerves or what, but it is not comfortable for the interviewer. If the interviewer is made to feel uncomfortable, nothing good will come from it. Be an active listener, meaning be alert and listen to what is being said and what is *not being said*. An example would be "The person who had this job wore a lot of hats and was a strong communicator who got along with lots of other groups that we interface with." What is not being said, but implied, is that we would like to have someone like him as *his* replacement. You should point out comparable strengths and times when you functioned in a similar role with multiple responsibilities sometime during the interview to take advantage of this information.

Never argue with anyone during an interview. If there is a difference of opinion about a particular topic, you can state your position, but never press it to the point of a heated discussion or an argument. You may appear to win the argument, but you will lose the job!

Finally, don't answer questions too quickly before thinking them out. No one will think ill of you if you take a moment to consider your answer. Quite the contrary, in most instances, you will be viewed as a person who is thoughtful, analytical, and who thinks before reacting. In days gone by, a common phrase for someone just quickly responding or acting too quickly was referred to as "shooting from the hip." Years ago, we had a number of cowboy references in our corporate speak. Instead of someone getting "blindsided," they were "ambushed." And we had a laundry reference. We were "hung out to dry," instead of being "thrown under the bus," as we say today.

Chapter 8

HOW COMPANIES MAKE THEIR HIRING DECISIONS

Naturally, hiring decision processes vary from company to company and can differ dependent on the position they are hiring to fill. However, there are several constants that are considered in all companies and environments. In small companies or businesses, the boss or owner tends to make the decisions but may ask input from existing employees to see if there will be any personality conflicts. I've worked at companies that had a well-constructed, formal process where each member of the interview team had to complete a form with questions about the candidate's suitability for the job. I've also worked in companies where there was a round-table discussion with each of the interview team members scheduled after the interview to evaluate the candidate. And in some other environments, the hiring manager would poll each of his team and afterward meet with his staffing representative (recruiter) to go over their evaluation and impressions of the candidate.

In cases where you're interviewing for a high-level job and the hiring manager has to get his upper-level management in the interview process, that individual's input is considered essential feedback in going forward or not. Generally, the higher up the chain of command an interview goes (unless it's a high-level, non-management type position), the more big-picture information is discussed and shared. The candidate will get an understanding of the organization and how it fits in with the company's high-level goals. The organization structure is usually drawn on a white board (commonly referred to as their org chart) to demonstrate the collaborative functionality of the company and their particular group's importance. Included in the importance of this team or department is the critical nature of the job you are interviewing for and why it is available. Since this is a high-level position, the talented professional chosen for it will have significant responsibility to add to the bottom line success of the company and hopefully enhance the skills and knowledge of the existing team members.

Sounds like big shoes to fill, eh? Darn right, but that's why you want this job. You've worked hard, learned much, and your experience has taught you meaningful lessons that you can apply *anywhere*. In addition to learning what *to* do, you've learned what *not* to do! You've been in charge and were successful under some trying conditions, but now you've pretty much stagnated in your current job, so this is your opportunity to regain that spark you lost some time ago by doing something challenging and exciting again!

So what are the criteria for evaluating a candidate that pretty much holds true in most cases?

First off, there is education, which doesn't mean you have to always have a particular degree or level of degree (bachelor's, master's, or doctorate), because there are many talented and successful people working in their area of expertise without a degree. But in certain areas, especially many of the engineering areas, an engineering degree gives you a foundation that includes engineering concepts, principles, and oftentimes, exposure to complex lab work to test and analyze current theories and practices. In finance and accounting, a degree in accounting is very valuable because knowing accounting principles and having other accounting knowledge can keep a company out of trouble with taxes while maximizing company profits. More times than not, you can be relied on to keep abreast of the company's investments and financial strength. In these days of mergers and acquisitions, accountants are invaluable to their companies.

That being said, companies realize that a number of bright go-getters may have had to interrupt their schooling to help support their family or some other life experience situation, so "equivalent work experience" is sometimes included in a job's requirements. For our purposes of decision-making, education is a plus, not a showstopper if you don't have it.

How important is communication? It's very important. You probably know talented people who cannot get their point across without verbally going through the woods and down the creek. Or what about people who can do most anything, but cannot describe the simplest of procedures? As you know, communicating is more than talking; communicating is influencing, presenting, clarifying, and persuading. In the staffing community, we suggest active listening in order to be in sync with the interviewee. When you're an active listener, you are able to hear what is being said and detect what is *not* being said. It's a skill that takes practice but is obtainable.

Try it in your conversation regarding something you know a lot about. Try listening more, instead of rushing to get your viewpoint across. Then try it again with some others who know something about the same subject. You'll hear that certain things are omitted that are important to the subject but are left unsaid or left to your imagination. Be careful that you don't start interviewing your friends instead of just talking with them.

During the interview, you'll be asked to describe, explain, and sometimes defend things you have stated on your résumé or about samples of your work you've brought along for show-and-tell. And if it's a group or panel interview, the questions come at such a rapid pace that you need to keep your wits about you just to keep up—and *still* give comprehensive, full answers. (If you have rehearsed and prepared for possible questions pertinent to the position, it will go a lot smoother for you.) Additionally, you will be asked to describe how you were able to successfully complete such a challenging assignment with so little assistance and limited resources. Know that your communication skills are on full display while answering.

Related or relevant experience. Pretty self-explanatory, wouldn't you say? That is, if you are interviewing for a job that you have experience in, written about on your résumé, and articulated what you've done in it during the interview. Remember this is one of those times where your preparation will serve you well. This is an area that you should have slam-dunked or triumphed in with no sweat. This portion of the interview is your bread and butter, because this is your area of expertise they're asking about. You're thinking, *Not only is my experience relevant to this job, I've excelled in this whole arena!* This brings us to another point.

Competence level of your skills and knowledge are objectively evaluated. Now that you've had your say at what you know and how well you know what you know, you will be evaluated on your level of competence of your ability and demonstrated skills. All of those behavioral and situational questions and discussions—working with others in and outside your area, your exposure to complex, leading-edge methodologies, processes, or system configurations, spreadsheets, database designs, time and motion studies, and whatever else may be specific to your area of expertise— will be graded and evaluated against what is acceptable in meeting the requirements of the job. In short, it's pretty much how you stack up with the requirements and with the description of the job.

Remember how I mentioned to study the job description carefully and to ask questions about it prior to coming in for the interview? Well, doesn't it stand to reason that the person who closely matches what the job is responsible for doing will be the candidate most likely to be seriously considered? This is important because requirements are generalized and don't necessarily reflect the experience of everyone. Some candidates have come up through the ranks, while others have had other paths and still ended up on the same level through education, and in some cases, by developing innovative ideas and implementing them. Regardless of how you gained your knowledge to be qualified, it's the execution of your duties and responsibilities that determined your success or not, which is exactly the core of the interview.

Leadership and interpersonal skills are what I refer to as the intangibles. They aren't always clearly defined, but they become apparent as you perform your duties. Attitude and personality play a big part in this area. If you've demonstrated a consistent desire for learning and adding to your skill set, taking it upon yourself to help your group become more productive by sacrificing some of your free time by working over lunch or after hours, you are demonstrating fine leadership qualities. If you are viewed as someone who's always willing to lend a hand to assist others, and you are always cool under pressure or when things go a bit haywire, you are quick to engage others in developing approaches to resolve tough issues or adjusting to changes in direction, then let's just say that you probably don't have a problem in the interpersonal area either.

Gone are the days when you could be the most talented person around but weren't required to interface with others, to contribute in meetings, to brainstorm, to give input on best approaches to proceed on an important project, to help solve a problem, or to help on some issue that was slowing down progress. It is now all hands on deck!

The other part of interpersonal skills is evaluated for "cultural fit" within the group. There are numerous "pushing the technology envelope type" environments that are so fast-paced and on the surface seem impersonal. Generally, those groups are constantly striving to make their products run faster, have more capacity, increase their durability, add more features and colors, become smaller, become more compact, become more attractive, become more streamlined, and overall improve upon them to outperform their competition. They constantly challenge themselves and each other, so it takes a special personality or someone with a real passion for that kind of work to do well in such an environment. As my good friend Darryl Bozeman would say, "All slow traffic to the right!"

Strengths may include strengths that you've claimed to have, but you would have to demonstrate your knowledge of them for the interview team to agree. These are the strengths that the interviewers feel you demonstrated with your responses and from the work you brought along to show and describe. Perhaps your response to one of the questions asking you to describe how you handled having to step in for your manager when she became ill and had to be hospitalized for several weeks to recuperate from surgery might be something that indicates your in-depth capabilities.

Strengths can withstand skepticism or doubt, are difficult to shake or loosen, and are apparent when searching for them. We all have some, but you must make them abundantly clear during your interview, especially if they are related to the position.

Weaknesses are next and often thought to be the flip side of strengths. Depending upon the requirements of the position, a weakness could be fewer years of working at something than the job requirement called for or that the company prefers (i.e., three years of management experience versus six years). Or it could be coding in a particular language for four years doing maintenance and design and development for only two years when the requirements called for more than three years of development. Other weaknesses could be that you haven't had actual work experience doing what this job will be doing. However, you studied it in school and spent hours in the lab working on similar tasks that are done in this job. Plus you've done well on the questions about things done and knowledge gained that you stated on your résumé. Other weaknesses include the areas that you may be decent in but want to master. So you are teaching yourself on an ongoing basis.

Sometimes, your enthusiasm and past performance in a different environment are enough for the interviewer to be sold on you. After all, every applicant (someone who applies for a job) or candidate (one who has been notified that there is interest in his application) is invited in for an interview because the company has decided that they're interested in learning more about that person as a possible fit for their job opening. Companies don't bring candidates in to practice interviewing or, as my ole friend Dick Fletcher would say, "for drill" but to fill openings.

One additional comment about enthusiasm: Please know that interviewers make a mental note of your energy level before and during the interview. Many an interviewer has remarked in writing or verbally about a candidate's lack of energy or how energetic or enthusiastic they were. Energy level is another indicator of one's possible behavior on the job. If you are lackluster or listless in the interview, when you are trying to make your best impression, what would you be like working there?

I can recall interviewing people who were slumped down in the chair and appeared to be bored with the whole interview process, yet they would tell me their coworkers would say they were "energetic and always helpful." Well, with their lack of energy and poor, unprofessional posture during the interview with me, they certainly didn't demonstrate much energy or enthusiasm to help anyone, *especially* themselves!

I think some candidates are so confident in their abilities (both real and imagined) that they think being energetic or showing enthusiasm isn't anything they need to do because their record of achievement speaks highly of them and reflects their excellence in a particular area or activity. Well, a piece of paper about your past performance cannot reveal your interpersonal skills or your cooperative, teamwork character. Nor does it give any indication of what kind of personality match you could be once on the team or as an employee. Good hiring decisions are extremely important because people spend many hours at work and oftentimes spend more time with fellow employees than with their family or loved ones. If there is a bad hire or a personality mismatch, the whole group suffers. Do not give an interviewer reason to discount your abilities as a qualified candidate because of being smug or arrogant, unnecessarily uncomfortable, or nervous.

Other, more job specific areas may include overnight or out of state travel or shift work, which could include some weekends; each could be a deal breaker for some. Remember having everything you want in a job is as rare as a Major League Baseball player having a 300 batting average for six years in a row while playing multiple positions (but mostly second base) like the late, trail-blazing, great All American Jackie Robinson. There will always be some manner that you'll have to stretch yourself in order to accommodate the job. For example, the commute could be farther than you'd like and you may have to cross a bridge or two, something you'd not do ordinarily. The first month you may have to travel overseas to meet with your foreign counterparts and learn their portion of the business. Or you may have to stay late every other Wednesday evening to be on the biweekly conference call of all the sales offices around the country. If in retail, you may have to rotate staying late to close the shop every other month; maybe there is a rotating training program where you go to other locations to train the company's business partners on the latest and soon-to-be available products. Perhaps there is a system that places each new member of the team to work with the swing shift group to learn the systems and processes quicker since it may be a slower, less hectic shift than the day shift.

We've all had to do something out of our preferred comfort area in our personal, professional, or school life at one time or another. When you look back on it, did you really *want* to take that literature course at 7:00 a.m., or would you prefer it to have been at 8:00 or 9:00? But you did take it and did well in it, so well that it sparked your interest in pursuing your own writing career. And you've been enjoying the career of a journalist ever since! That is, until your company had a massive layoff and went out of business. All of that caused you to now be interviewing at one of your former competitors. But take heart, because when one door closes, another one opens even wider.

Recap instructions: Go back and read over each of those areas carefully. Mentally digest them, and refer to them as you continue your job quest.

Chapter 9

INTERNAL JOB SEARCH OR INTERNAL TRANSFER

For those of you who are currently working but want a position with more responsibility, more direct management responsibility, or just something different with more challenge, let's discuss the process involved and how to go about getting what you want.

Most of us know someone or have experienced for ourselves when our current job no longer excites us. Before we find ourselves dreading to go to work each day, which is a big difference compared to when we would wake up before the alarm went off some years ago—full of excitement to see what the workday would offer. Now we feel like the alarm goes off way too early and our job has lost its luster. We may feel stagnated, unappreciated, and nearly invisible because our position seems insignificant in the overall scheme of things. The promises made early on about upward mobility "with countless opportunities in any direction you choose" seem to be a distant, vague memory of time long gone. Well, before you put your résumé together and start reaching out to friends and business contacts in your network, do your proper due diligence at your current company.

Typically, companies have periodic review or evaluation schedules in place. They are designed for you and your boss to meet to go over your work performance and to set your goals for the next cycle of work. Some companies conduct their review/evaluations semiannually, some quarterly, and some annually, while others may conduct them on the anniversary date of your hire. Regardless of when they occur, you should include some discussion about your career goals. Perhaps you want to move up the ladder or head up something. You should discuss with your boss what is required in order to move into that next step or position. If you find yourself in an environment where a regular review or evaluation (sometimes referred to as a "focal review") schedule is not adhered to and you seldom meet with your boss except during business strategy or staff meetings, you may want to become more proactive regarding your career desires.

If you don't have regular one-on-one meetings with your boss, you need to request a meeting to discuss your career. Usually at work, there are telephone calls or email messages streaming in nonstop and would prove to be too much of a distraction for such an important discussion. It would be best and more effective if you were to have it outside of his or her office. A quiet restaurant that is not the local eating spot where most of the company's employees go to lunch would be desirable to reduce the interruption possibilities.

For those of you who have completed or are in the midst of completing a degree, obtaining a certificate of successful completion of anything that is relevant to the performance of, and additional knowledge of your job, you should definitely include in any career discussion. Although they would like to think they are more active than they are in developing the careers of their staff, management for the most part do a lousy job in this area. Therefore, you must take the initiative to help them help you. You'll need to express what you want and how you plan to get there.

Since you've requested the meeting, you must set the agenda and the talking points. It would be a good idea to bring a list of things you've contributed, goals accomplished, special or unique things you've added to the group or company since you came on board. It's remarkable how many people forget significant achievements or contributions after they are no longer critical.

Regarding your accomplishments, you may want to compare them to others who have been promoted or given additional responsibilities. While your focus may be on your career, don't forget to point out how the company will benefit by your promotion or by receiving broader responsibilities. Companies save money and time by promoting from within because their employees already know how the company works, even more so than what their official systems and processes would suggest, because they know the human factors: the go-to reliable people and those who get things done quickly and efficiently. On top of that, the time spent in the interview process takes time away that the interview team could be getting work done. Plus regardless of how talented and bright the outside hire may be, there is still some "come up to speed" time required for them to be productive.

As much as you may be admired, within a business setting, the business comes first. I've known fellow employees who schmoozed or sucked up to their bosses on such a regular basis that they were totally shocked when they were notified that their contracts weren't going to be extended or that they were being let go. While they were busy sucking up and thinking they were buds, they should have been working toward being tops in their respective areas of responsibility.

I once worked with a fellow recruiter who spent so much time developing his filing system with colorful file-folders—going from pastels to more vibrant and bolder shades of about four color groups—while he was less than urgent in filling openings, which was what he was hired to do. Granted, his files were the most colorful I had seen, but they didn't safeguard his job, and his contract was short-lived.

During the meeting with your boss, you want to convey that you are interested in making a move into something more challenging where you can continue growing and learning. Ask them where they see you heading in the company or organization. You'll need to know what skills are required for it. Will there be classes you could take? Is there in-house training available? Could your work schedule be adjusted to accommodate evening classes or early morning classes if available?

Now none of this is relevant if your boss says that he or she does not see you in a different (or better) position in the future. In that case, ask them what areas you need to improve upon in order to get their support in going forward in your career. Ask if they would be supportive of you transferring internally in a position that might match your background. As you can tell, this discussion is very pivotal to your longevity at your present job and will give you a good indication of what your boss thinks of your work and capabilities.

Unfortunately, some bosses may want to keep you in your present role because they've grown accustomed to you doing your job without them having to do much managing. Plus they may choose to not go through the work of replacing you.

Some people apply for an internal transfer and decide not to tell their current boss about it until after interviewing for it. Well, guess what. Whether you work for a small, medium, or large company, your current boss will be notified when you apply for another position inside your present company. For medium to large companies, your HR rep will be notified to check to see if you are on a PIP (performance improvement plan) or not.

This brings me to a rather important aspect of this whole process, one that is of immense importance. You must be doing a good job in your current job if you want to be given more responsibility, a promotion, or a lateral, internal transfer. Most companies have rules stating that you must have been in your current job for a year and are in good standing and not on a PIP in order to be considered for an internal transfer. I'm sure you would agree that no one wants to take on an employee who has been a problem or who has had problems getting their work done. Although managing is part of their responsibility, most managers would choose not to have a potential problem to manage or fix.

After discussing your accomplishments, your desires, and after receiving the constructive critique of your work from your boss, try to establish either a schedule or next steps toward what you two agree on. If there is no agreement as to what you want and what they see for you, or if they are unwilling to support your efforts toward your career goals, then you know it's time to move on. To be fair, there may not be any openings or opportunities that match your background throughout the company—in the foreseeable future. Your boss may greatly appreciate your work, your ideas, and your expertise in your job but may not have anything more to offer you. If that is the case, do the very best you can in your present job, while confidentially embarking on your job quest. Please continue to do your best because you want (and need) to have good things said about you, your work ethic, demeanor, and productivity when reference checks are conducted. And please don't assume that your new employer will never talk with anyone in your current company or organization just because you didn't include any of them in your list of references. Know that more times than not, someone will know someone who knew you when you worked there, and your final days there are what usually stand out in their mind.

The Counter Offer

You have successfully landed an offer from another company. That's right: "successfully landed," because until you receive an offer, you're just one of many in the interview process. But once you receive an offer, you're now in the game! In some cases, you'll be in the driver's seat, depending on how badly they want you.

Let's say that you received the offer, but after doing the math, including the stock options, the restricted stock, the quarterly or annual bonuses, etc., you needed a bit more since the longer commute would add more wear and tear on your car, more gas, tolls, and additional child-care expenses. Most candidates would also take into consideration their upcoming raise, gifting of stock, bonuses, and other perks they enjoy at their present company that they'd be giving up. Some companies pay for club memberships, may offer a pension or retirement plan, and other retention programs that add to their total compensation.

Like most salary or compensation negotiations, you'll get some things and not others. For example, you may get more stock options but a lower percentage on the quarterly or annual bonus since those are usually governed by corporate rules and regulations. You may get a little more in base salary, maybe even a sign-on bonus that you receive within your first few weeks after starting to work at your new company.

Sign-on bonuses are generally given to make up the difference of what the candidate desires and what the company wants to give them. Sometimes, it is offered when the candidate is making a base salary or has a comp package that is so high in the salary range that anything over it would put them in a different bracket or salary range. There are instances when anything over their salary would put them over the top performer already working there. Let's say the candidate is making $85,000 and wants a 10 percent increase to take the job, but the top-performing and highest-paid employee working there already is making $92,000. Well, $85,000 + 10% is $93,500 and over the top performer's salary. If this position is really vital and the company really wants this candidate, it may offer him or her a smaller salary increase (say $87,000) and a one-time sign-on bonus of $8,000. Everyone is happy and the company hasn't offered a salary higher than their super star's salary to an unproven, new employee!

Okay, now we've had the staffing person or recruiter go back and forth checking with HR, or in some cases their own records of the current team's compensation. And he or she has compared the selected candidate's background, education, and potential to the existing team members or employees and obtained the necessary approvals to go forward with formalizing the offer, including the sign-on bonus. Then the offer is extended. Well, guess what. The satisfied candidate, who most likely has been sharing all of this activity with his or her spouse, after getting what they want, is ready to submit his or her resignation. Naturally, the candidate gives a two-week notice to their current boss, meaning they have officially resigned and will be leaving the company after two weeks.

Their boss reacts as if they've been struck with a lightning bolt or received a hard punch in the stomach! This is pretty common, because it comes as a surprise. More importantly, their boss hasn't planned for this occurrence. His or her immediate thoughts are *Who can I get to replace _____ (this employee)? What will happen to the stuff they are working on? What will happen if we can't meet our goals? This could affect my bonus! I can't let him or her go. No way!*

Afterward, your boss will contact *his* boss or the owner of the business to share the bad news and to see how far they might be willing to go to keep you from leaving. Generally, people whom you haven't seen in a while, sometimes people you thought hardly knew you existed, would call you or come by to see you. All of a sudden, you become very popular with people telling you how wonderful you are and how surprised they are to hear that you want to leave. You could be invited out for fancy lunches, even drinks after work with the gang.

After a few days, your boss will want to have that serious talk about your future with them and your current company. He or she has gotten permission to match your offer from the other company and will tell you of the exciting plans the company has for you, including a promotion in the near future. Other things that you may or may not have mentioned you wanted in the past could also be promised. You will be reminded of the times you had family-related issues or an illness where you had to take off early or needed to take a couple of days over your allotted sick day allocation that your boss approved for you. Instances are brought up about your solid teamwork and how you singlehandedly accomplished something significant for the company. In effect, you can't leave such a good situation where everyone appreciates you and recognizes your outstanding talent and skill set! "Come on! We're like family here!"

Important: If you had your one-on-one discussion about your future and your career desires already and had come away less than enthusiastic regarding your future with "them" and your current company, you will see through this "corral dust" (as my pal Apache Corral calls it) and realize that it's not really about you. However, if you haven't done your due diligence before embarking on your job search, you will no doubt be blown away with all the attention and the over-the-top accolades. Heck, if you didn't know better, you'd start thinking that you were indispensable! And why would you want to leave anyway? You've got friends here, you're familiar with how things get done, you understand the politics of the place, and they have matched your offer along with some promises of additional things in the future. If you stay, you'll obviously please many people, and heck, you may not like that other company or that *other job* after all! You talk it over with your spouse again, and with your impassioned input, you two agree that you should stay put.

Sorry, Charlie or Charlene. Wrong decision! It took your threatening to leave before you were recognized as an important asset of the company. Do you find it a bit odd that they are willing to match your offer, in effect giving you an increase out of the review/evaluation cycle? Did you do anything special for it? No, you were going to leave and then people came out of the woodwork to influence you to stay. You'll notice after the dust settles that you are looked upon differently. You're not asked to sit in on all of the key meetings like before. Whenever you're on the phone or on your computer, you feel like you're being eavesdropped on or that your computer is being monitored by the IT folks. Not much later, there could be resentment toward you from your colleagues or even your boss. They may feel that you only used the threat of leaving just to get more money and promises made when you had no intention of leaving in the first place! Yes, you will get the raise and may eventually get some of the other things promised, but they will be slow in coming. You have declared yourself untrustworthy for long-term advancement in this company. You can't be relied on as one of the team. You might decide to bolt again when things don't go as fast as you'd hoped. You might prove to be difficult to manage, because you can no longer be trusted. Were you actually ill when you took those sick days or were you out interviewing again? Did your family really experience those events that required your immediate, prolonged attention, or were you interviewing then too? Even those friends of yours that you enjoy working with and having lunch with on a regular basis have changed toward you. Although still cordial with a few jokes here and there, they seem to be less chummy. They too think you got away with a fast one. A few of them may even remark that they should use your method for getting a raise, a promotion, or whatever you got that resulted in you being put on the company's fast track.

As you can see, it's never a good idea to accept the counter offer. You are damaged goods; you have shown your "hold card." You made known what others have kept to themselves and then you reneged when you got what you wanted. You were out hunting wild boar, but when you had one in your sights, you couldn't pull the trigger. In effect, you weren't committed to leaving; you merely wanted recognition, praise, or whatever!

Now let's continue with next steps.

You now have to let the other company know that you are reneging on your acceptance of their offer. In addition to the hiring manager and his or her team being shocked and disappointed, the staffing person or recruiter is crushed—and angry. They worked diligently to schedule interviews around your schedule, gave you critical feedback on your résumé and your interview skills, got answers to your questions that weren't covered during your interviews, went to bat for you in the selection process, and put in the extra effort in order to contact those key executives with full schedules who needed to approve your compensation package—all to accommodate you! Depending on their level of professionalism or personality, they may label you a flake and make it known that you should never be considered for a job at their company ever again. They may have harsh words for you and your indecisiveness, your lack of integrity, etc. Or, you may hear things like "Sorry it didn't work out this time, but I'll touch base with you in a few months to see how you're doing. But in the meantime, we have a critical opening still and I'd really appreciate you referring someone you know to be a good fit for the position."

We obviously can imagine what will happen to this candidate within a year's time, so it's no use scolding someone who has just put a big target on their back. I've known candidates who were calling back after two to three months to see if that job was still available. I guess the counter offer had soured already and their life of hell had begun. We still have a job to fill, however, and since they are feeling a bit remorseful by reneging on their word (acceptance), they may feel better about themselves if they can refer someone to us, the recruiters. (Think about it. Who knows what it takes to land this job better than the person it was offered to?) And well they should; they've created a problem for us because we had a deal and now we need to begin the hiring process all over again.

But let's back up a minute. What if you do not accept your present company's counter offer? Well, they might offer you even more and perhaps a promotion because they still don't want you to leave. If you turn down all of their counter offers, it is very likely that your boss will ask you to "at least give us some time to find or train your replacement" or to ask you to complete all of the important tasks or projects you're working on. What they're really saying is "Give us more time to work on turning you around." If you know that your departure in two weeks will put them in a bind and you're certain that your mind is made up, I would suggest you give your current boss a three-week resignation notice, but no more.

It's always good to try to complete your major responsibilities and to clean up any backlog tasks while in the interview process. Therefore, you will not leave your company in a lurch, nor will they be able to ask you to stay on for a long time until those things are completed.

Internal Transfer

Like any job that you want, you need to be qualified. Approaching a job internally, like your external job search, it helps to know someone. Unless you work in a very large company, more often than not, you will be familiar with someone who works in the area that you are attracted to. The attraction can stem from the potential challenge of the duties of the job, the potential broadening of your skill set, or possibly the potential step toward management. These are all valid reasons and are positive steps along your career path. Your reputation, past performance, and accomplishments are of paramount importance when you pursue something in house.

But it is, to use an overused metaphor, a double-edged sword, because the good news is that many people know you or know of you, and the bad news is that many people know you or know of you. If you're known as a person who is well meaning, conscientious in their work, willing to help out when necessary, and overall brings a positive attitude to work on a consistent basis, you will stand a much better chance of getting what you want than someone who has a less positive approach and a distant personality. If you find yourself in the latter grouping, you'll need to work on yourself. Ask your current boss if there are areas you could improve upon, and you should observe your successful colleagues. Study their work habits, including their interaction within your group and outside of it. Notice how others respond to their opinions; in essence, check out the credibility they enjoy from others. Think of a meeting comprised of people with differing and opposing views and bordering on flat-out failure to come up with a solution or an approach that everyone can agree on. All of a sudden, one person speaks up, offering a logical suggestion that touches on several different points of view that appears to be the solution. That person is the type of employee everyone wants in their group. They usually are active listeners, respectful of others' opinions, open to new ideas and approaches to things, and generally command respect because of their in-depth knowledge of something relevant to the subject matter. Be that person!

Chapter 10

SEARCH FIRMS AND
EMPLOYMENT AGENCIES

You will sometimes respond to a job posting that was posted by a retained search firm or by an employment agency. Retained search firms typically handle executive level positions, are retained by the company to fill critical openings, and are given exclusivity in doing so. They generally get paid about 33.3 percent (some even more!) of the first year's salary and total compensation package, which could include a sign-on bonus, stock options, restricted stock, executive bonus, etc. of the selected or placed candidate. They get paid in three installments: one third of the fee after signing on to take the search, another third paid after thirty days, which can coincide with presenting several possible candidates, but not necessarily, and the final third paid upon placement of the final candidate.

Retain search firms usually have a long relationship with their client companies and specialize in their client's industry or are specialists in a needed discipline at the executive or "C level" (chief executive officer, chief financial officer, etc.). They pretty much act as an extension of their clients, since they conduct detailed interviews around the qualifications of the position and their suitability to the corporate culture of their client's company, including psychological profile evaluations. They are generally good at making those decisions, because they have oftentimes been the search firm that hired the existing or prior members of the client company's officers and top executives. Companies choose to hire search firms for their critical senior-level openings rather than use their topnotch, in-house recruiting talent, because the outside search firm can approach their competitors directly for possible candidates. They seldom need much start-up time and can begin searching right away. And like most other recruiters/headhunters/staffing professionals who are always trying to identify and recruit top talent, they usually have easy access to a number of high-level, capable candidates in their database to begin contacting. I have found that as successful as they may appear, there are always high-level, topnotch professionals who are interested in learning about any solid career opportunity that matches their background and keeps them moving forward along their career path.

Employment agencies or contingency search firms can sometimes have an exclusive for a position and even exclusivity on a number of positions for a short period, from a client company, but generally do not. Companies feel that they can get more résumés from several contingency search firms than with just one. Since the payment terms are vastly different from retained search firms, it makes good business sense for them to do so. The kind of candidates they generally are assigned to produce are anywhere from talented professionals with a few years of experience to midlevel managers. Or simply candidates with leading-edge, pushing-the-technology-envelope backgrounds or bright hard-chargers in other areas who will make fine bankers or financial analysts and other talent that is in hot demand in their particular business or industry. In some instances, the company could be growing so rapidly that they don't have the time or the in-house staffing resources to bring on a lot of people at once—regardless of their backgrounds or demand in the marketplace. I can recall some years ago, when there were several search or placement firms that did 80 to 90 percent of their business hiring nurses because there was such a high demand for them.

Contingency search firms usually charge anywhere from 20 percent to 35 percent of the selected candidate's first year's salary and can also include their first year's projected bonus as part of their fee. Instead of their fee being paid in three installments like the retained search firms, contingency search firms only get paid after the selected hire starts work. Thus, their fee is paid contingent upon hiring the candidate and after that candidate starts working. A reduced-fee arrangement occurs when there are multiple openings that are given to a contingency search firm to fill. I've seen fees as low as 15 percent per hire for a group of openings (usually eight to ten or more) that were negotiated and agreed to in order to get exclusivity on filling all of them. Again, the same advantage of a client company having someone else approach top talent from their competitors and the contingency search company recruiters specializing in the areas needed to fill those critical openings. As for all of those résumés of candidates not chosen to hire or even interview, the client company now has more résumés to refer to for future hiring needs.

Some contingency search firms have made it more challenging for those client company staffing folks to easily reconnect with their presented candidates in the future by omitting the contact info and in some cases the name of their most recent employer on their résumés. This only makes the savvy (in-house) recruiters dig a bit more, but they can usually locate the key candidates they are interested in pursuing. Generally, any hires made with any of those candidates after an agreed amount of time—say six to twelve months—are usually free of any fees to the contingency search firm.

A third outside hiring source is the temporary staffing firm or temporary agency, often referred to as a temp agency. These search firms place talented professionals on a short-term basis, usually when their client company's regular employee will be off from work for a while. These temp assignments are available when a person in a critical role goes on vacation, a maternity or paternity leave, or even a sabbatical in some cases, but not as often as years ago.

A number of prominent companies in Silicon Valley used to offer a six- or eight-week sabbatical after so many years of continuous service to their key, usually management-level, employees. They started having problems when those same employees would add their vacation time to their sabbatical and would be out for several months. Some got so accustomed to the time off and away from the constant pressure of achieving their ambitious, company goals, or having to attend an endless number of meetings, plus enduring their long commutes, that they decided they didn't want to come back! Several persons in high-level management positions, I was told, even made demands on what they would require to come back to work. I heard that one person demanded a promotion before they would return. It got so troublesome that most companies that offered a sabbatical simply dropped it from their corporate benefits. I'm starting to see several start-ups offering sabbaticals again. We'll see how long they last *this* time.

Temp agencies charge their client company an hourly rate for the services of their temp worker, contractor, or in some cases referred to as a consultant. They in turn pay the temp worker an hourly wage, generally without any company benefits, whether they work in a full-time or part-time capacity. There are exceptions to this with some of the larger, well-established temporary search firms who offer some employee paid benefits at competitive prices after working on an assignment for a number of hours, but there is seldom any bonus pay for the successful temporary worker.

There are obvious pros and cons working as a temporary or contract employee. First off, the assignments are not permanent or as long lasting as a regular, full-time position. There are no company-paid benefits, nor can they participate in an employee stock purchase plan like they could if they were company employees. However, temporary workers can often work hours as they see fit, get paid for overtime, and enjoy flexibility in their work schedule. Plus they have an opportunity to work in a variety of company environments and to add those work experiences to their arsenal of skills and knowledge.

Not sure if you are aware of it or not, but many recruiters or staffing consultants are contract or temporary employees. They're usually hired on a three-month contract to assist in hiring. If they are successful and there is an ongoing hiring need, their contract gets extended. I've known competent contract recruiters who have worked over four years at companies that had significant growth or high turnover. Some successful recruiters are offered a regular or company employee position, especially if there are ongoing hiring needs.

In addition to temporary agencies offering temporary work assignments, they sometimes will have temp-to-perm assignments. One of *those* assignments could be the entry into a regular job at a company where they would enjoy working as a company employee. (Companies no longer use the term "permanent job" or "permanent employee" but "regular job" and "regular employee." This is because there is no longer permanence in employment with so many companies with at-will employment, shipping functions overseas or out of state, or being an active participant in the game of big fish swallowing up smaller fish—merging with another company, causing some employees to become redundant or duplication in their job function, aka excess.)

Now that we are clear on what the most common search firms do and how they differ, let's engage with them properly.

All recruiters, whether working inside as an employee of a company, working outside as a retained search or in a contingency search capacity, or as a contractor working for a limited time, are working to fill openings. Each of them has specific positions and requirements that must be met in order to successfully fill those critical openings. Although you may not be selected for the first opening they may contact you for, you should certainly keep in contact and establish a good business relationship with them. I say "them" because it behooves you to have a good relationship with several recruiters, because they have different career opportunities in different companies and sometimes even cover different geographical regions. Since we all know of someone who has relocated from one place to another for a business opportunity, it is almost expected that many of us will have to do so for our career at some time or another.

One of the suggestions I make to students is to master their primary language and to learn an additional one to become even more marketable to a prospective employer. Plus you open up your chances of opportunities when you can speak and write in other languages, because we live in a global economy where corporations have business interests around the world. Knowing how important it is to communicate effectively in all functions and business situations, one must work night and day honing one's communication skills until one is sharp and effective. Not having good communication skills is like giving someone directions to a place without knowing the names of the streets or highways that would get them there. You might be talking, but not saying much. When I was a teenager living in New Jersey, there was a song with lyrics that said "talking loud, but saying nothing" that comes to mind. LOL.

Also, keep your recruiters up to date on changes in your background (i.e., obtaining college degrees, getting a promotion, hitting your company goals, being recognized for outstanding performance, adding some leading-edge technical training, getting a teacher's credential, acquiring special training offered by your current employer, or completing your PMP (Project Management Professional) certification, which opens the door to obtaining a project management position and earning a higher salary than those without it.) It's important because the additional skills, knowledge, or experience can be just what you need to be seriously considered for a new, exciting career opportunity.

Finally, regarding those illustrious firms that specialize in hiring, do what you can to get a face-to-face meeting with the recruiters you choose to assist you in your job search. When you're only a voice in their voicemail or over the telephone, or a person behind an email, you don't have the impact on them that you could have in person. In person, you can present yourself as the professional person you are while demonstrating your commitment or passion for the kind of work you are seeking. Plus you want as many allies in your job search as you can get. And inside allies are invaluable, if you can get them!

Suggestions

Get to know who you are dealing with when you decide to get assistance in your job pursuit.

Establish a partnering relationship because you both need each other to be successful in your respective areas of responsibility. The recruiter needs to identify the right job, and you need to do well in the interviews and get the job.

Be honest with them, tell them the companies where you have already applied or interviewed, so they won't waste time presenting you there again.

Be clear on what you want to do and where you will go to work—and not.

Part 4

Chapter 11

REFERENCES

Susan Miller's Astrology Zone (Susan's horoscopes, planetary formations, and movement interpretations are some of the most popular in the world; 43 percent of her readers live in America, and the rest are spread across the United Kingdom, Canada, India, Brazil, and Turkey), in her monthly horoscope reading for April 2014, says,

> A recent survey from Career Builders reported that 62 percent of the references that people list on their applications spoke negatively to the inquiring employer about the applicant. A total of 69 percent of the employers who called a person's list of references reported that they changed their mind about hiring the applicant.

First of all, I was blown away by that number when I read it. Knowing how important references are in things related to hiring, why would candidates be so careless with their references? After you've put in the time and effort to do well in your studies, learned and mastered difficult aspects of your job to succeed in challenging environments that required you to work long hours and even weekends, while sacrificing for you and your family's future, why would you give references that will say negative things about you? You might as well just say that you don't really want the job and withdraw your application.

Please know that your references are *almost* as important as your interviews. References are validating what you have stated on your résumé, what you said during your interviews, and are a confirmation of the interviewer(s) impression of you! Since you have furnished contact info and names of present or former colleagues, bosses, or satisfied customers that you worked with directly or indirectly who can speak to your competence and work ethic or habits, it is presumed that they will have positive things to say about you. And depending on the job, certain questions are pretty standard (i.e., ability to work in a team and/or independently, your organizational skills, aptitude, and adaptability, ability to multitask in a fast-paced environment, job knowledge, cooperation, judgment, work habits, quality of work, quantity of work, communication skills, initiative, creativity, dependability, honesty, and integrity). In addition to those, companies want to know in what areas you've demonstrated your core talents and ask questions about your major strengths and, conversely, the area that you should continue to improve upon. (Yes, some of these were asked and discussed during your interviews. So now you see the connection and why it is so important to select your references with considerable care.)

Sometimes we assume that everyone sees us the way we see ourselves, but that is a false assumption. Those times when you ardently participated in meetings sharing your knowledge and asking questions for clarity before moving along, some of your colleagues thought you were grandstanding and posturing for the boss. When you regularly insisted on getting answers to things that others felt you could have taken "offline" after the meeting, you were perceived as being self-absorbed with little regard for the rest of the department or group and their time.

Another aspect of our work character that sheds a negative light on our performance is when we overpromise and underdeliver. I guess you know that it should be the other way: underpromise and overdeliver. Remember, it is business and not something casual. Keep your word no matter what you have to do. If that means working late, coming in earlier, working on the weekend, whatever it takes—because you said you would deliver!

On those rare occasions when you absolutely cannot do what you said you would do, take the time out to speak to the person you made the promise to and let them know when you will be able to keep your word. I would bet that most of us who've been a member of a project team in school or in an actual work environment have experienced some form of inconvenience or disappointment by someone we worked with not coming through as they had promised. Usually it's on something time critical. What is really galling is when they showed surprise when we expressed our dissatisfaction because they had put us in a bad light, usually to those who depended on us to come through.

I can recall awaiting a promised return call on an important hire regarding the offer that was out of the guidelines and required upper-management approval. Well, the would-be approver was at a different location, miles away from my office, but only several feet from my staffing colleague's office, who routinely prided himself on rubbing elbows with and getting approvals from high-level executives in the company. Well, I waited, and I waited, and I even waited some more because I had the candidate on standby to receive the approved offer to take home over the weekend to discuss with his wife. Yes, it was a Friday afternoon that turned into evening before I finally left. I received a weak response and a half-apology from the offender the following Monday.

Think of the times you were told that certain things would be done by a certain day or after so many hours—only to be disappointed and sometimes inconvenienced because you developed your schedule in accordance to what you were told. Now that I think about it, similar behavior patterns probably were practiced by many of those applicants who had their references say negative things about them!

I was fortunate to have worked with some talented and good people over the years, but I had my share of challenging characters as well. Some of them made great statements or promises at planning meetings for some special event or activity, even volunteering for critical tasks, but later were no-shows or would beg off the day before and drop their tasks onto others. As I reflect on them, they seemed to enjoy hearing themselves talk and would make verbal commitments that didn't connect to their actions after the meetings were over. More times than not, your promises will influence the work of others, and if you don't hold up your end, others will suffer.

Don't be one of those people! As the old Creole expression goes, "I'll be slow to lie." Don't impulsively make promises that you will regret later.

A harmful habit that many people have is to become lackadaisical after deciding they've burned out on a particular job and mentally check out once they start looking for a different one. Guess what. Your workmates notice that behavior, especially if they have consistently counted on you in the past. Once you connect with another company and complete the interviews and are selected for the job, you probably will use several of those same people as your references. Perception is a powerful thing. (My late, dear, very wise grandmother would often say, "A good name is better chosen than riches.") Always maintain a stellar reputation.

One more important thing is to keep in touch with your references periodically so that they know that you are still in the job hunt and are alerted to possible calls from potential employers. No one wants to be surprised with a call from a company representative asking them about someone they worked with that they haven't talked to in months or longer. The uneasiness doubles if the job you've interviewed for is different from what your reference remembers you doing when they worked with you! It's very difficult for them to speak to your management abilities and style when they've only known you as an individual contributor. I've had to give references on people whom I worked with in one capacity and they were interviewing for a very different job or on a different level or concentration. Had we not kept in touch over the years and discussed what they were doing, I would have been a less effective reference for them. And as the survey at the beginning shows, references can be very critical to you getting a job—or not!

In conclusion, be careful with your selection of references, keep in touch with them with updates on your professional life, and ask if there are things you can do to help them or their family members. Some may have recent grads that need helpful career tips or an intro into a company you may have personal contacts with. Always offer to return a favor, and don't hesitate to tell them about a business opportunity you think they are qualified for or might have interest in doing. (You never know. Your references may be seeking a better or different position also!)

After a relatively short time, you'll realize how important solid business contacts and good references are to your career growth and longevity. There are times you will encounter the "Who do you know?" bridge. The one that you need to know someone before you are invited to step on it. Be advised these are professional relationships, so do not badmouth people you work with or voice undue frustration over things that generally every professional person faces. And do not—yikes!—show signs of being a whiner in conversation with your references. In short, your communication with them should be similar to your behavior and responses during an interview. Be professional!

Recap

Don't take the reference thing lightly. References can help or torpedo your successful job search.

Give them reasons to endorse you wholeheartedly.

Cultivate your relationship with your references; don't just contact them when you need something. Offer your contacts and other resources they may need.

Be respectful of their help. Give them a heads-up beforehand about possible calls and who may be calling and why.

Chapter 12

OVERCOMING THE ISMS

Unfortunately, as if trying to land the right job for yourself isn't difficult enough, there are the isms you must contend with as well. There are racism, sexism, and ageism, to name the most prevalent ones. Although some people would have us believe that we live in a color-blind society, there is overwhelming evidence to the contrary.

So what do we do when it confronts us during our job quest? Well, we typically have to demonstrate in word and deed that we are qualified not only to do the job but also to become a productive member of the team or company. Most prejudicial and racial attitude is based on ignorance or fear. As a job applicant who is on time, well versed in the subject matter, well prepared for the interview process and the questions that may be asked, and engages effectively in the interviews—answers questions honestly and to the best of your knowledge and ability—you begin to dispel those baseless presumptions and prejudgments. Will you sometimes feel that you aren't given the benefit of the doubt on some elementary-sounding questions, given your level of education or experience? Yes, but you should certainly answer those questions and add a comment that speaks to your deeper knowledge of that area. Will there sometimes be veiled insults during an interview? Yes again.

I was interviewing for a contract recruiter position with a top international company to hire sales and marketing people, and each of the interviews up to the final decision-maker had gone exceedingly well. Meaning each of them had read my résumé and asked very good questions about specific environments I had worked in, how I managed particular challenges, what were the results and what were the lessons learned, what hiring processes I found most effective and which ones I thought cumbersome and why. I say these are good, because the purpose of an interview is to learn about the applicant and not to assume what they may or may not know or what their individual involvement was, simply from their résumé.

Well, the final decision-maker was a young, jeans-wearing director who looked at me in amazement. I guess no one had bothered to tell him that I was an African American or that I was over thirty-five. (I had seen a number of late twentysomethings and young thirtysomething folks passing through the lobby while I was waiting to be brought into the interview, but the people I interviewed with were older and we had a lot in common businesswise.) Well, each time he asked me a question and I answered it, he would say, "Yeah, that's right" or "Yeah, that makes sense." But later during the interview, he started adding "man" to his comments, "Yeah, man." This surprised and perplexed me, since this wasn't two guys talking over a couple of beers but a formal interview with the director of the group I would be working in. And although pleasant and upbeat, I did not encourage anything less than a formal, fact-seeking interview session.

As he wrapped up what seemed to be an abbreviated interview, he said, "Well, man, it's obvious you know your stuff. I want to thank you for coming in." Nope, I never heard back from him, and when I called back after a few days, I was told the job had been filled.

So what did I learn from that experience? I should have asked if there was anything more he needed to know from me, when did he expect to make a decision, and where did I stand in that decision. But frankly, there were too many negative signs that I saw from the director, signs that shouted he would be extremely difficult to work with and I would probably have to reeducate him about folks who have a "perma-tan" as I jokingly referred to my complexion in those days. Perhaps, I would have to teach him how to work closely with someone older than him. Or worse, since he was the big honcho, he might feel that he could take undue liberties and tell stereotypical racial jokes in my presence, which would have been a *big* problem.

For those of you referred to as the "baby boomer" generation, the perception is that you are inflexible and think you know everything already, that you are incapable or unwilling to learn new approaches or systems that may be more efficient than the ones you worked with, or that you may want to take your boss's job. Au contraire! Most of the baby boomers that are still in the workforce have demonstrated their flexibility by keeping current on the more efficient systems and processes. And not only learning them but training their colleagues junior to themselves so that they will be knowledgeable and become more productive. Plus they usually have firsthand, historical knowledge (not to mention their vast experiential knowledge!) that enables them to avoid wasting time experimenting with bad assumptions or theories.

Think of that parent or relative of yours who said, "I don't want you to make the same mistakes I made." And in this economy of fewer job opportunities than in past decades, most baby boomers are happy to still be employed and doing what they love doing. They typically want to share their knowledge and their experience while gaining more of each. As for wanting their boss's job, they have usually done that *and got a T-shirt, the sweatshirt, and the cap!* Plus more times than not, more seasoned employees have already spent time *married* to a company in the past—attending early morning meetings, staying late to work on critical projects, and in most cases, doing their share of working weekends as well.

In essence, they've paid their dues and focused on their career, making it their most important aspect of their life—in the past! At this stage in their career, they want to contribute and help the present (working) generation be successful in whatever capacity that's needed. They usually still have a passion around their work and simply enjoy doing it.

The other benefit that comes to mind is that the more seasoned employees can set the stage for how others react to change: change in direction, change in deadline, change to a new location due to growth and expansion, change in leadership, even change in work assignments. When the perceived, well-established, seasoned employee supports the changes, the rest of the group follows suit. So it is wise for the manager or leader of the group to establish a good relationship with them rather than be paranoid that they want his or her job. It's always puzzled me that managers don't realize that the more talented and accomplished their team is thought to be is a direct reflection on their leadership, hiring, and management ability. Surely, they should see that a well-run, productive staff gives them time and energy to devote their attention to planning and strategizing for the future. I guess that is why some environments give workshops on "managing upward," or managing their bosses.

Sexism is a bit tricky but just as reprehensible. It was so prevalent some years ago that I would receive résumés with the applicant's first name replaced with initials. Some female applicants didn't want to be prejudged, discounted, or even eliminated because of their gender. This was especially true in the more technical and manufacturing areas when the so-called "good ole boy" network was in control and wanted to keep it that way. Since I became familiar (and fascinated) with the technical areas and manufacturing processes that went hand in hand, I was able to assist in changing those attitudes and practices of exclusion over the years. Human resources personnel became advocates for those changes, and we would tell hiring managers and their bosses that they needed to get their numbers up regarding more women or whatever group was underrepresented according to the EEOC or other federal government guidelines.

With all of that said, there are still dinosaur-thinking employers mired in the past. They say things like "We've never had a woman in this role before. How do you think you will get along with the other employees?" Although it should be incumbent upon the existing employees (including the hiring person) to make the new hires welcome and to integrate them into their team, some interviewers ask the candidate to convince them that they will fit in and ask how they would go about it.

Instead of being put off by this question, use it as an opportunity to state your experience where you demonstrated your flexibility and your self-motivation to be successful. Naturally, mentioning how you voraciously read everything available related to your past job, worked long hours, asked insightful questions of your colleagues while getting to know them, and after a short while was able to contribute in several critical areas and ultimately became a valued go-to person in the company is a fine way to respond.

The bottom line is that the emphasis is on the bottom line. Companies want to develop expandable systems and processes, produce good products that people want, maximize their profits, and create an environment that attracts bright, talented people who want to carve out a career with them. That being the case, companies must welcome a diverse mind-set, and with their minds comes diversity in many forms. "It's nobody's business," in the words of Billie Holiday, "what I do." "Outside of work," I'll add. But seriously, who you love or choose as your life partner has no bearing on how you perform your job. So keep your private and personal life to yourself, unless you want to invite your workmates to opine on it. If not, treat your workplace like it is: a workplace and not a social gathering. As you may know, there are people with personalities that believe they are supposed to pass judgment on any and everything that others say or do. Deprive them of feasting on information about you, except your work-related activities.

Regarding age discrimination, some people in the job market or who are still working shave their graying beards and moustaches off, dye their hair, and work out regularly to maintain a slimmer, youthful appearance, so that they won't be penalized because of their age. (I know a hair salon owner in his sixties who works out at a gym three days a week, dyes his hair to eliminate his gray, and gets facials on a regular basis to maintain a youthful-looking, clean-shaven face so that his wealthy clientele will keep patronizing his business while he flirts with them. He says that nothing "un-professional" ever happens with any of his clients, but his attention to his appearance must be working because his business keeps flourishing.) I've read where women have mixed their funky-looking military or hiking boots with their business apparel or wear funky jeans with a blazer to appear hipper and younger in order to better fit in. All I can say is "I'm sorry that you feel you have to do those things, but do what you think is best." For those of you who might wonder what industries tend to hire older workers, I read in the *AARP Bulletin* (March 2014) that "healthcare, education, financial services, government, and nonprofits" valued the experience of workers "over age fifty." It probably hasn't changed that much since.

Be aware of the dragons lying in wait, but don't let them stop you or turn you away from your goals.

Chapter 13

ESTABLISHING OR BROADENING YOUR PROFESSIONAL NETWORK

So you don't have any business contacts, nor do you know how to go about getting any. Then read this carefully: Buy a newspaper and read every article in the business section. Pay close attention to the recent promotions listed, because they are usually indicators that those companies are growing or reorganizing. In either case, they are signaling a change within their business environment and may very well need some additional talent like you.

If one or more of the people mentioned work for companies in your area of expertise, background, or simply the area you want to work in, see if you can contact them. A congratulatory email or phone call would break the ice of you being a stranger to them. Naturally, you will give them a five- to eight-second summary of who you are and that you would greatly appreciate any help they might provide for you to follow in their footsteps. Do not oversell, don't be pushy, and be respectful yet determined and focused. This is where your active listening skills can be utilized. Pay attention to what they say. If they talk of being terribly busy, suggest another time for a brief phone call to speak in more detail, but only about five to ten minutes, max! If that goes well and you are able to have a subsequent call, you will want to shoot for a fifteen-minute face-to-face meeting in their office or over coffee at their favorite breakfast spot before going to work.

Another method is to go on one of the popular job websites and type in a company name that you are interested in working for or want to get firsthand information about. You've probably heard of some sites where current and former employees share their opinions about their employers, both pro and con, and although informative, they won't cast as wide a net as you need for networking purposes. Once you put in the name of the company, many profiles or people working there will appear for your viewing pleasure. Read through the profiles to see what positions or backgrounds match what you have done or would like to do. Depending upon the site's guidelines or procedures, contact those people who you would like to know or those you think could be helpful in your job search. Write a succinct message telling them of what you two may have in common and what your intention is for contacting them. Do not be disheartened if you don't get a quick response, because working people in today's market are very busy working the equivalent of one and a half to two jobs. Remember, however, a bit of flattery sometimes goes a long way. If someone has been struggling with some complicated work issue or feeling overwhelmed with so much on their plate and happens to see a message from you that is complimentary, interesting, and succinct, you just picked up their day! Each week, take a different company and repeat the contact procedure until you no longer need to do so.

For those of you who have recently graduated from college or completed a program specializing in your field of interest (IT, nursing, real estate, carpentry, construction, etc.), contact former graduates who are working in your field to pick their brain and to get introduced to their contacts. You have your school in common and most likely have the same burning interest to do similar work, so these connections should go swimmingly well. In picking their brain, try to get information about organizations that are active in your area of interest. There may be online chat rooms, alumni associations, trade unions, pre-apprenticeship and apprenticeship programs—a host of memberships too numerous to mention that you can participate in or join.

The next suggestion that comes to mind is to attend conferences, job fairs, and even conventions if possible. Experts or highly successful people in your area are there to present the latest and greatest of products, processes, opinions, theories, practices, etc. With a little bit of maneuvering, you'll be able to approach them and introduce yourself.

Again, after introducing yourself and a brief summary of who you are and complimenting them on a fine presentation, mention something about a talking point in their presentation or their work that you're familiar with to start the *short* conversation. At the conclusion of your *short* conversation, requesting a business card or contact information from them is not out of bounds. If you repeat this and come away with three or four experts' business cards or contact info at the end of the event, you are very successful. That is, potentially successful. You'll still need to follow up with them to cement a solid relationship.

A solid relationship may not be forthcoming for a while, depending on their schedule and what may be happening in their lives, but if you are able to receive several pointers from experts in your chosen field, their advice could very well prove to be invaluable and worth gold in the time they will save you.

Finally, ask your relatives, friends, former instructors, counselors, everyone you have career-related conversations with about people they know in a hiring function, or someone with contacts that you can utilize to help get you in the door. People of various stages in their careers get referred to me all the time. Some become paying clients, and some are relatives of friends that I counsel or help in some manner for free. I've discovered throughout my life that the good I do for others comes back to me in some form or another tenfold. If it doesn't get reciprocated to me directly, something good happens to someone close to me: my wife, my children, and my friends. As the saying goes, "It's all good."

Summarizing

Sometimes establishing or broadening your network is similar to an exploratory interview, but not always. When you are expanding your network, you are establishing relationships that will have regular and hopefully frequent communication between the two of you. Typically, there will be things in common, although sometimes an age difference, similar interests exist. No one achieves their dream job or works in (or on) what they are passionate about, without the assistance of others. After landing your job, if you consistently give your best in performing your duties, your professional network will likely grow at all stages of your career. You too will get calls from bright wannabe's that need just a *few* minutes of *your* time.

CONCLUSION

Know that your quest for a J-O-B is not an easy undertaking. There will be disappointments, rejections, and false promises that will nearly cause you to give up in exasperation. You must not let any of that stop you on your journey to find and secure the job you want. Listen to your inner core, and be motivated by what you truly want to do. We are all put here for a purpose, some with multiple purposes, so identify yours and go for it.

Put in the time. Invest in what it takes. Education, specialized training, and even new languages might be required, but you can do it. My dear, deceased father, one of the most successful and disciplined men I was privileged to know, would achieve things that others said were impossible and then do them again so that the first time wouldn't be thought of as luck. He was driven to succeed in all that he did because he was taught to always do his best. His best was usually better than the rest.

Train yourself to remember names, faces, and backgrounds. Think of the times when someone remembered your name and how good it made you feel. Think how impressed you were with the person who remembered it. Perhaps you had only met them once before and for only a short time. You want to be remembered for good things, things that have you stand out from the crowd or from the ordinary. You want to be known as that person who is forthright in his or her communication, focused on your career, while willing to assist others on their own career journey.

Once you adopt good habits of keeping your word, being honest, working hard and often smart, while helping others in the process, you will grow in your career as a responsible contributor, and you may find yourself on a management tract without even realizing it. In addition, but just as important, our society will benefit as well.

Just remember to properly PREPARE!

Proceed. Put your thoughts into action.

Research. Do background work on the company and its industry.

Evaluate best approaches to utilize.

Position yourself to succeed.

Accept your shortcomings and work to improve.

Reflect on past challenges and successes.

Excel by always doing your best!

> One important key to success is self-confidence. An important key to self-confidence is preparation.
>
> —Arthur Ashe

ABOUT THE AUTHOR

Solari Jenkins is a senior-level staffing/ employment professional with over thirty years of interviewing, hiring, mentoring, and counseling professionals on various aspects of their job searches and career paths. He's worked in major corporations as a consultant, contract recruiter, technical recruiter, staffing specialist, staffing manager, senior staffing manager, and director of staffing. He has also worked in employment agencies and was co-owner of a search firm (Jenkins & Kilcullen Inc.), which he helped develop and was its philosophical leader, setting the tone while developing and implementing the operational aspects of how it conducted business.

Since developing a passion for employment early on, Solari has devoted most of his professional life learning how to be an effective, successful employment specialist without losing his soul. He takes pride in bringing integrity to every recruiting assignment or consulting position he's engaged in, big or small. He believes having a good working relationship with an employment expert is as important as having a good lawyer to call upon!